THEORISTS OF THE MODERNIST NOVEL

In the early twentieth century the modernist novel exploded literary conventions and expectations, challenging representations of reality, consciousness and identity. These novels were not simply creative masterpieces but also crucial articulations of revolutionary developments in critical thought.

In this volume Deborah Parsons traces the developing modernist aesthetic in the thought and writings of James Joyce, Dorothy Richardson and Virginia Woolf. Considering cultural, social and personal influences upon the three writers and connections between their theories, Parsons pays particular attention to their work on:

- forms of realism
- the representation of character and consciousness
- gender and the novel
- concepts of time and history.

An understanding of these three thinkers is fundamental to a grasp of modernism, making this an indispensable guide for students of modernist thought. It is also essential reading for those who wish to understand debates about the genre of the novel or the nature of literary expression which were given a new impetus by Joyce, Richardson and Woolf's pioneering experiments within the genre of the novel.

Deborah Parsons is a senior lecturer and chair of postgraduate programmes at the University of Birmingham, UK. Her principal interests are in Modernism and visual and urban culture.

ROUTLEDGE CRITICAL THINKERS

Series Editor: Robert Eaglestone, Royal Holloway, University of London

Routledge Critical Thinkers is a series of accessible introductions to key figures in contemporary critical thought.

With a unique focus on historical and intellectual contexts, the volumes in this series examine important theorists':

- significance
- motivation
- key ideas and their sources
- impact on other thinkers.

Concluding with extensively annotated guides to further reading, *Routledge Critical Thinkers* are the student's passport to today's most exciting critical thought.

Already available:

For further details on this series, see www.routledge.com/literature/series.asp

THEORISTS OF THE MODERNIST NOVEL

James Joyce, Dorothy Richardson, Virginia Woolf

Deborah Parsons

LONDON AND NEW YORK

First published 2007 by Routledge
2 Park Square, Milton Park, Abingdon, OX14 4RN

Simultaneously published in the USA and Canada
by Routledge
270 Madison Ave, New York, NY 10016

Reprinted 2008

Routledge is an imprint of the Taylor & Francis Group, an informa business

Typeset in Perpetua and Helvetica by Taylor & Francis Books
Printed and bound in Great Britain by TJ International Ltd, Padstow, Cornwall

British Library Cataloguing in Publication Data
A catalogue record for this book is available from the British Library

Library of Congress Cataloging in Publication Data
Parsons, Deborah L., 1973-
  Theorists of the modernist novel : James Joyce, Dorothy Richardson, and Virginia Woolf /
Deborah Parsons.
    p. cm. – (Routledge critical thinkers)
  Includes bibliographical references.
  1. English fiction–20th century–History and criticism. 2. Modernism (Literature)–Great
Britain. 3. Joyce, James, 1882-1941–Criticism and interpretation. 4. Richardson, Dorothy
Miller, 1873-1957–Criticism and interpretation. 5. Woolf, Virginia, 1882-1941–Criticism and
interpretation. I. Title.
  PR888.M63P38 2006
  823'.91209112--dc22
                              2006022249

ISBN10: 0-415-28542-9   ISBN13: 978-0-415-28542-1 (hbk)
ISBN10: 0-415-28543-7   ISBN13: 978-0-415-28543-8 (pbk)

CONTENTS

SERIES EDITOR'S PREFACE

The books in this series offer introductions to major critical thinkers who have influenced literary studies and the humanities. The *Routledge Critical Thinkers* series provides the books you can turn to first when a new name or concept appears in your studies.

Each book will equip you to approach these thinkers' original texts by explaining their key ideas, putting them into context and, perhaps most importantly, showing you why they are considered to be significant. The emphasis is on concise, clearly written guides which do not presuppose specialist knowledge. Although the focus is on particular figures, the series stresses that no critical thinker ever existed in a vacuum but, instead, emerged from a broader intellectual, cultural and social history. Finally, these books will act as a bridge between you and their original texts: not replacing them but rather complementing what they wrote. In some cases, volumes consider small clusters of thinkers working in the same area, developing similar ideas or influencing each other.

These books are necessary for a number of reasons. In his 1997 autobiography, *Not Entitled*, the literary critic Frank Kermode wrote of a time in the 1960s:

On beautiful summer lawns, young people lay together all night, recovering from their daytime exertions and listening to a troupe of Balinese musicians. Under

> their blankets or their sleeping bags, they would chat drowsily about the gurus of the time . . . What they repeated was largely hearsay; hence my lunchtime suggestion, quite impromptu, for a series of short, very cheap books offering authoritative but intelligible introductions to such figures.

There is still a need for 'authoritative and intelligible introductions'. But this series reflects a different world from the 1960s. New thinkers have emerged and the reputations of others have risen and fallen, as new research has developed. New methodologies and challenging ideas have spread through the arts and humanities. The study of literature is no longer – if it ever was – simply the study and evaluation of poems, novels and plays. It is also the study of the ideas, issues and difficulties which arise in any literary text and in its interpretation. Other arts and humanities subjects have changed in analogous ways.

With these changes, new problems have emerged. The ideas and issues behind these radical changes in the humanities are often presented without reference to wider contexts or as theories which you can simply 'add on' to the texts you read. Certainly, there's nothing wrong with picking out selected ideas or using what comes to hand – indeed, some thinkers have argued that this is, in fact, all we can do. However, it is sometimes forgotten that each new idea comes from the pattern and development of somebody's thought and it is important to study the range and context of their ideas. Against theories 'floating in space', the *Routledge Critical Thinkers* series places key thinkers and their ideas firmly back in their contexts.

More than this, these books reflect the need to go back to the thinkers' own texts and ideas. Every interpretation of an idea, even the most seemingly innocent one, offers its own 'spin', implicitly or explicitly. To read only books on a thinker, rather than texts by that thinker, is to deny yourself a chance of making up your own mind. Sometimes what makes a significant figure's work hard to approach is not so much its style or content as the feeling of not knowing where to start. The purpose of these books is to give you a 'way in' by offering an accessible overview of these thinkers' ideas and works and by guiding your further reading, starting with each thinker's own texts. To use a metaphor from the philosopher Ludwig Wittgenstein (1889–1951), these books are ladders, to be thrown away after you have climbed to the next level. Not only, then, do they equip you to approach new ideas, but they also empower you, by leading you back to a theorist's own texts and encouraging you to develop your own informed opinions.

Finally, these books are necessary because, just as intellectual needs have changed, so the education systems around the world – the contexts in which introductory books are usually read – have changed radically, too. What was suitable for the minority higher education system of the 1960s is not suitable for the larger, wider, more diverse, high-technology education systems of the twenty-first century. These changes call not just for new, up-to-date, introductions but for new methods of presentation. The presentational aspects of *Routledge Critical Thinkers* have been developed with today's students in mind.

Each book in the series has a similar structure. They begin with a section offering an overview of the life and ideas of the featured thinkers and explaining why they are important. The central section of the books discusses the thinkers' key ideas, their context, evolution and reception: with the books that deal with more than one thinker, they also explain and explore the influence of each on each. The volumes conclude with a survey of the impact of the thinker or thinkers, outlining how their ideas have been taken up and developed by others. In addition, there is a detailed final section suggesting and describing books for further reading. This is not a 'tacked-on' section but an integral part of each volume. In the first part of this section you will find brief descriptions of the key works by the featured thinkers, then, following this, information on the most useful critical works and, in some cases, on relevant websites. This section will guide you in your reading, enabling you to follow your interests and develop your own projects. Throughout each book, references are given in what is known as the Harvard system (the author and the date of a work cited are given in the text and you can look up the full details in the bibliography at the back). This offers a lot of information in very little space. The books also explain technical terms and use boxes to describe events or ideas in more detail, away from the main emphasis of the discussion. Boxes are also used at times to highlight definitions of terms frequently used or coined by a thinker. In this way, the boxes serve as a kind of glossary, easily identified when flicking through the book.

The thinkers in the series are 'critical' for three reasons. First, they are examined in the light of subjects which involve criticism: principally literary studies or English and cultural studies, but also other disciplines which rely on the criticism of books, ideas, theories and unquestioned assumptions. Second, they are critical because studying their work will provide you with a 'tool kit' for your own informed critical reading and thought, which will make you critical. Third, these thinkers are critical because they are crucially important: they deal with ideas and questions which can overturn conventional understandings of the world, of texts, of everything we take for granted, leaving us with a deeper understanding of what we already knew and with new ideas.

No introduction can tell you everything. However, by offering a way into critical thinking, this series hopes to begin to engage you in an activity which is productive, constructive and potentially life-changing.

WHY JOYCE, WOOLF AND RICHARDSON?

'[O]ne great part of every human existence is passed in a state which cannot be rendered sensible by the use of wideawake language, cutanddry grammar and goahead prose', James Joyce declared while writing *Finnegans Wake* (*LJJ* III: 146). 'I remember . . . my astonishment when Pointed Roofs was greeted as a "Novel"', Dorothy Richardson said of the publication of the first instalment of her thirteen-volume life's work *Pilgrimage* (*LDR*: 496). 'I have an idea that I will invent a new name for my books to supplant "novel"', Virginia Woolf wrote in her diary in 1927, 'A new ? by Virginia Woolf. But what?' (*D* III: 34). In her nine novels, innumerable critical essays and reviews, and extensive autobiographical writings, Woolf persistently explored and experimented with the boundaries of literary convention in order to express more fully the qualities and intensity of conscious experience. If Joyce and Richardson were less prodigious in terms of the quantity of their fictional and critical writings, they made up for it with the vast length and uncompromising inventiveness of their key works. Yet what was it about the model of the novel as they inherited it that so dissatisfied them? And, as Woolf deliberated, what would they put in its place?

The early twentieth century marks a significant moment in the history of the English novel, its status and future becoming a matter of constant literary debate as both writers and reviewers questioned how the form and subject-matter of modern fiction should respond to the shape and experience of modern life. To the contemporary reader the novel may seem one of the most resilient and mutable of literary forms, expansive (or vague) enough in definition to include a vast range of styles and sub-genres. In the early 1900s, however, it seemed to many young writers, James Joyce, Virginia Woolf and Dorothy Richardson among them, that the best-selling novels of the day had become stuck within fixed and limiting rules for the representation of character and reality. For a generation born into the last decades of the Victorian era, yet whose maturity coincided with technological innovation, scientific revolution and the destructive rupture of world war, the sense of living in a new age was acute, and what had become the conventional forms of fiction seemed inappropriate, even hostile, to the depiction of their contemporary moment.

'On all sides writers are attempting what they cannot achieve,' Woolf wrote in an essay titled 'Poetry, Fiction and the Future' (reprinted as 'The Narrow Bridge of Art'), 'forcing the form they use to contain a meaning which is strange to it' (*E* III: 429). That meaning was a picture of existence newly shaped by the revelations of Darwin, Freud and Einstein among others, and that in its disturbing implications prompted 'monstrous, hybrid, unmanageable emotions':

> That the age of the earth is 3,000,000,000 years; that human life lasts but a second; that the capacity of the human mind is nevertheless boundless; that life is infinitely beautiful yet repulsive; that one's fellow creatures are adorable but disgusting; that science and religion have between them destroyed belief; that all bonds of union are broken, yet some control must exist – it is in this atmosphere of doubt and conflict that writers have now to create . . . (430)

Such bewildering ideas both stimulated and posed new problems for imaginative representation. Modern life could not be fully expressed in the form of lyric poetry, Woolf argues, which was unsuited to the rendering of everyday realities, nor that of the current novel, all too happy when portraying details and facts but awkward and self-conscious when attempting to convey a sense of the profundity of life and being. The novel of the future, she advocates, would need to combine the two, possessing 'something of the exaltation of poetry, but much of the ordinariness of prose' (435):

> It will make little use of the marvellous fact-recording power, which is one of the attributes of fiction. It will tell us very little about the houses, incomes, occupations of its characters; it will have little kinship with the sociological novel or the novel of environment. With these limitations it will express the feelings and ideas of the characters closely and vividly, but from a different angle. . . . It will give the relations of man to Nature, to fate; his imagination; his dreams. But it will also give the sneer, the contrast, the question, the closeness and complexity of life. It will take the mould of that queer conglomeration of incongruous things – the modern mind. (435, 436)

At the same time, she demands, the new novel will 'be written standing back from life' (438), so that the writer can compose its common complexity into the rich import of art. Formally radical, subjectively real and aesthetically autonomous, expressive of a world in which the present seems dislocated from the past, experience is fragmented, multiple and limitless, and previous certainties about the physical world and our selfhood within it have been swept away; this was the art that Joyce, Woolf and Richardson sought to create. The result was the development of what has been variously described as the 'psychological', or 'stream-of-consciousness' or 'modernist' novel.

PIONEERS

While sharing an aim to convey aspects of human existence typically unrepresented by conventional prose, along with certain formal stylistic similarities in the ways that they did so, the material social and cultural contexts from which Joyce, Woolf and Richardson thought and wrote were very different: Joyce an Irishman self-exiled to Europe, single-mindedly pursuing his extraordinary craft while supported and feted by the most forward-thinking patrons of the cosmopolitan art world; Woolf the product of Victorian upper-middle-class liberalism, her work nurtured within the context of high-brow Bloomsbury aesthetics; Richardson a staunchly independent 'new woman', pioneering her revolutionary 'feminine' prose on far less than the five hundred pounds a year that Woolf would famously declare necessary for a woman to be able to write.

Joyce, Woolf and Richardson have all been well-served by biographers, and for the fullest accounts I point readers towards Richard Ellmann's *James Joyce* (1959; rev. 1982), Hermione Lee's *Virginia Woolf* (1996) and Gloria Glikin Fromm's *Dorothy Richardson: A Biography* (1977). The first two were both born in 1882 (coincidentally they also died in the same year, 1941), Joyce into a family of rapidly declining prosperity in Dublin during the political climate of the Parnell years, Woolf into the inspiring milieu yet restrictive social respectability of the Victorian upper-middle-class intelligentsia. Despite increasing poverty as a result of his father's improvidence, Joyce's education was undertaken at prestigious Jesuit establishments (Clongowes Wood College, a boarding school in County Kildare, and then Belvedere College in Dublin). By the time he was studying languages and philosophy at University College Dublin, however, he was desperate to escape what he regarded as Ireland's moribund parochialism and narrow Catholic nationalism. He went to Paris in 1903 to study medicine, but returned after only a few months to be with his dying mother. In 1904 he began work on some sketches of Dublin life (finally published as *Dubliners* in 1914), as well as an autobiographical novel *Stephen Hero*, but the city now seemed to the young Joyce more stagnant than ever before. In the middle of June he met Nora Barnacle and together they left Dublin for good, settling first in Trieste, where Joyce worked as a teacher of English, and later in Zurich and Paris.

Joyce always had difficulty in placing his work with mainstream publishers, who were hesitant about its lack of mass-appeal and arguably libellous and obscene content. By 1913, however, the manuscript of *A Portrait of the Artist as a Young Man* had come to the attention of the American poet and exuberant champion of modernism, Ezra Pound, who worked energetically to secure the patronage of Harriet Shaw Weaver and its serial publication in the avant-garde literary journal of which she was editor, *The Egoist*, in 1914 (it was published in book form by B. W. Huebsch in America in 1916). *A Portrait* was received by the majority of reviewers (favourably or unfavourably depending on their point of view) as literary realism taken to crude yet dazzlingly inventive extremes, but few recognised any hint of the meticulous and multi-layered compositional order with which Joyce would endow that realism in his next work. The first thirteen of the eighteen chapters of *Ulysses* appeared in *The Little Review* between March 1918 and December 1920, before the publication of the 'Nausicaa' episode resulted in it being banned for obscenity in both the United States and UK (a decision not overturned until 1933).[1] Encouraged by Pound, Joyce now moved to Paris, where the American bookstore owner Sylvia Beach offered to publish the novel under the auspices of her shop Shakespeare and Company, with printing subsidised by advance subscriptions. It finally appeared in book form in 1922, the complexity of the novel's style and vision, supported by some skilful marketing and its cult aura as a 'banned' manuscript, turning Joyce into a literary celebrity and confirming his elevation in the eyes of reviewers from the gutter of vulgar naturalism to the heights of the literary avant-garde.

Joyce himself was characteristically less than modest about his achievement. '[T]he value of the book is in its new style' he wrote to the musician Arthur Laubenstein in 1923 (Ellmann, 1982: 568). The influence of the narrative and structural innovations of *Ulysses* on modern fiction is incontrovertible. The novelist Ford Madox Ford wrote on its publication: 'Certain books change the world. This, success or failure, *Ulysses* does: for no novelist with serious aims can henceforth set out upon a task of writing before he has at least formed his own private estimate as to the rightness or wrongness of the methods of the author of *Ulysses*' (Deming, 1970: 129). T. S. Eliot took a more apocalyptic line, announcing to Virginia Woolf that *Ulysses* 'had destroyed the whole of the 19th Century' (*D* II: 203). For her part Woolf thought the novel 'an illiterate, underbred book . . . the book of a self taught working man . . . egotistic, insistent, raw, striking, and ultimately nauseating' (189). There was yet as much implicit rivalry as explicit genteel distaste in her response. On Eliot's recommendation the Woolfs had considered publishing *Ulysses* in 1918 through their own small publishing house the Hogarth Press, but finally refused, ostensibly due to its length, although more probably because they had been unable to find a printer who would agree to work on a manuscript so liable to prosecution for obscenity. Of Eliot's erudite enthusiasm for the novel Woolf remarked somewhat ruefully in her diary, 'He said nothing – but I reflected how what I'm doing is probably being better done by Mr Joyce' (69). His experimental approach she from the first found exciting, and was arguably a significant influence on the structure and form of *Mrs Dalloway* (1925). She was also prepared to acknowledge his accepted genius on the authority of those such as Eliot whose opinions she respected. What she found wanting in Joyce's work, however (as she also did that of Richardson), was its rendering of the self-absorbed mind, which failed to capture what was in her view the permeability of consciousness and relativity of identity.

Woolf was the third of four children (Vanessa, Thoby, Virginia and Adrian) born to Leslie Stephen, founding editor of the *Dictionary of National Biography*, and his second wife Julia Duckworth. Due to her sex and class she was precluded from the Cambridge education of her brothers, depending instead on voracious reading of the contents of her father's library. At fifteen she suffered the first of several breakdowns, the result of emotional strain caused by the deaths of both her mother in 1895 and her half-sister in 1897, the consequent estrangement of her father, and the sexualised attentions of her half-brothers. The following years were punctuated by periods of ill-health, and dominated by frustration and rebellion against the exacting emotional demands of a man she would remember with ambivalence as 'the tyrant father'. When he died in 1904 the Stephens quickly moved from the family home in Kensington to bohemian independence in Bloomsbury. If as a child Woolf had been surrounded by eminent Victorians, as a young adult she now revelled in lively and forthright discussions on art and politics with her brother Thoby and his Cambridge friends (among them E. M. Forster, Lytton Strachey, John Maynard Keynes and Woolf's future husband Leonard Woolf). The so-called 'Bloomsbury Group' was heavily attacked in the politicised literary critical climate of the mid-twentieth century for what was regarded as its exclusive and elitist ideology. Woolf's reputation suffered in consequence, although she herself typically refused any suggestion of its influence on her writing. Yet for the support of her developing sense of identity as a writer in the years between her father's death and her marriage to Leonard Woolf in 1912, the uninhibited and critically constructive environment that the Bloomsbury circle provided cannot be underestimated. The value of early Bloomsbury for Woolf was perhaps ultimately twofold; psychologically, in the emotional support it provided after the death of Thoby from typhoid in 1906, and creatively, in the emphasis on freedom of thought that was more prevalent in its discussions than any mutual aesthetic doctrine. The questions that she posed about the relationship between art and life in her regular reviews for the *Guardian* and *Times Literary Supplement* at this time were stimulated, if not answered, by the social, political and aesthetic debates of Bloomsbury.

Woolf was also by now struggling with the writing of her first novel, revising it repeatedly during several years of almost constant mental instability. *The Voyage Out* is a story of self-discovery, in which the sheltered Rachel Vinrace, journeying to South America with her father, aunt and uncle, is awakened to the possibilities of her imaginative and intellectual life and its suppression by the demands of a male-dominated world. Becoming engaged to an aspiring writer, she shortly afterwards catches a fever and dies, an ending that leaves tantalisingly hanging the question of whether, in death, the excitements and possibilities of Rachel's life have been cut short or its fears and limits transcended. It is partly the enigma that Rachel thus remains that Lytton Strachey recognised made the novel so 'very, very unvictorian' (Majumdar and McLaurin, 1975: 64). While she bears some comparison with the young Woolf in her frustrated yet eager embrace of perceptual experience, so too, however, does her fiancé Terence Hewet, the potential novelist, whose experimental vision suggests the possibilities of Woolf's own. When he comments, for example, that while male novelists constantly write about women, 'we still don't know in the least how they live, or what they feel, or what they do precisely' (*VO*: 245), he indicates a sensitivity to women's everyday lives and sense of self with which she would be constantly concerned, in both her fictional and non-fictional writing. His occasional belligerence indicates that he is not a straightforward vehicle for Woolf's views, but his comment to Rachel that 'There's something I can't get hold of in you' (245), and his desire to 'write a book about Silence, . . . the things people don't say' (249), are identifiable with her own fascination with the elusiveness of character and her attempt to find new forms for the novel that would allow for the expression of all that remained silenced within in its conventional limits.

The Voyage Out was finally published by Duckworth in 1915, along with another first novel by a woman writer, Dorothy Miller Richardson's

Pointed Roofs. It was the first instalment of what would become her thir-teen-volume novel *Pilgrimage*, a fictionalised account, through its quasi-autobiographical protagonist Miriam Henderson, of the thwarted prospects, trauma, depression, hard work and creative determination that had characterised her own life from the 1890s to 1912.[2] Richardson had been born into the leisured comfort of an aspiring middle-class family in Abingdon near Oxford in 1873. One of four daughters but always treated by her father as the 'son' of the household, she was educated at the pro-gressive Southborough House, where she studied both literature and logic, learnt French and German, and was introduced to the new disci-pline of psychology. All this changed with the financial crisis brought about by her father's poor investments, and at seventeen Richardson decided to earn her own living by taking up a position as a student teacher in a school in Hanover, Germany. With the weak mental health of her mother becoming increasingly apparent, however, she returned after six months to another teaching job in north London. In 1893 her father was finally declared bankrupt and the family moved to Chiswick, Richardson taking a post as a governess. In 1895 her mother committed suicide, cutting her throat with a kitchen knife while on a short holiday with her daughter in Hastings.

Following the horror of this event, Richardson moved to London, taking up employment as a dental secretary in Harley Street. The work was long and monotonous, but provided a structure and routine that had been swept away from her family life. Moreover she embraced the finan-cial self-sufficiency afforded by her meagre salary. Living in cheap lodg-ings in Bloomsbury, she revelled in the stimulation of life on the fringe of the social, political and aesthetic bohemia of the city in the late 1890s, although she refused commitment to any of the organised socialist, spiri-tualist or suffragette groups with whose theories she dallied, always remaining staunchly faithful to the social and emotional individualism that she had at first been enforced to accept. The impoverished yet entrancing London years form the context of the middle volumes of *Pilgrimage*, odes to the city in which Miriam's bond with its enveloping yet undemanding streets persists beyond the otherwise brief acquaintances or transient friendships of her urban life. Three relationships, however, did begin to dominate: with Benjamin Grad, the Russian fellow lodger who proposed to her; with Veronica Leslie-Jones, the adoring friend whom she would encourage him to marry; and with H. G. Wells, the husband of a school friend, and with whom Richardson embarked upon a long and animated intellectual affair. Their battles of opinion, particularly over such subjects as Fabianism, feminism and literary realism, sharpened her critical thinking on the relation of women and fiction, and stimulated and encouraged her own desire to write.

The emotional entanglements of Richardson's personal life, along with the combined stresses of an unplanned although not unwanted pregnancy, miscarriage and overwork, eventually brought her close to collapse. As she wrote in a note to Sylvia Beach in 1934, however, she had for some years planned a novel on 'the inviolability of feminine solitude, or alternatively, loneliness' (*JP*: 281) and she finally decided to resign from the dentists' surgery and attempt to make a living from her writing. Breaking from Wells, with the marriage of Grad and Leslie-Jones she moved to live from 1908–12 in a Quaker community in Sussex, writing sketches and articles for the *Saturday Review* while attempting to begin her novel. At first she was frustrated by her inability to represent her theme, a young woman's struggle to self-identity amidst the masculine domination of late-Victorian society, and discarded several first attempts. Looking back she recalled that the requirements of the novel form 'seemed to me secondary to something I could not then define, and the curtain dropping finalities entirely false to experience' (*JP*: 139). Finally, in 1913, she produced *Pointed Roofs*, rejecting the conventional demands of plot and character for an uncompromising focus on her autobiographical protagonist's own point of view. Edward Garnett, the reader who accepted it for publication with Duckworth, described it as a new 'feminine impressionism' (Fromm, 1977: 77).

The first volumes of *Pilgrimage* appeared rapidly, and by the time that *Interim* was serialising in the avant-garde literary journal *Little Review* alongside Joyce's *Ulysses* Richardson was at the highpoint of her reputation as a pioneer of the new 'psychological' novel. By the end of the 1920s, however, the books were taking increasingly long to write, and Richardson's audience were beginning to despair of Miriam's life ever reaching a conclusion (particularly when every long-awaited love interest or proposal seemed destined to be turned down). With the publication of

J. M. Dent's multi-volume *Pilgrimage* in 1938, which brought together the previously published eleven books with the addition of *Dimple Hill*, readers understandably assumed they had reached the final instalment. Richardson was devastated by this misrepresentation of her project, and continued to work on a thirteenth and final volume, *March Moonlight*, which takes Miriam up to the point of Richardson's meeting with Alan Odle, the artist she would marry in 1917 (it appeared posthumously in 1967). A decade older than Joyce and Woolf, she had survived them by a further sixteen years.

MODERNISM AND THE NOVEL

The task of introducing any moment within literary history is necessarily a selective one, and many writers influenced or contributed to the contested critical debate on the modern novel in the 1910s, 1920s and 1930s whose names punctuate the following pages but are impossible to include in detail. Henry James, Joseph Conrad and Ford Madox Ford, for example, were arguably the forerunners of a 'new' realism in the novel, while Arnold Bennett, H. G. Wells and John Galsworthy became its notable adversaries, as in a different sense did E. M. Forster, D. H. Lawrence and Wyndham Lewis, consciously evolving their own independently experimental strategies against what they viewed as the overly self-conscious and inward-looking work of Joyce, Woolf and Richardson. While all of these writers would have regarded themselves as writing a new 'modern' prose, none, however, would have thought of themselves as 'modern*ist*', a literary critical paradigm evolved and employed subsequently by the academic institution. The purpose of this guide is not to rehearse the surveys and scholarly criticism of modernist ideas and movements so available elsewhere, but to help the contemporary reader situate his or her developing understanding of the early twentieth-century novel within the context of Joyce, Woolf and Richardson's own thought and experimentation. In the following chapters we will explore the evolution of their specific aesthetic principles and thematic concerns, setting these within the context of the social, historical, philosophical and artistic ideas that influenced them. At the same time I hope to indicate their relative positions within the formal and social *politics* of the

MODERNISM

The beginning of the twentieth century witnessed an international revolution in the arts, as a wide range of cultural groups, aesthetic movements and individual writers and artists sought to extend and transform their relationship with and representation of reality. The word 'modernism' represents the retrospective fusion of these very diverse aesthetic experiments into the comprehensive style or social and psychological temper of a 'modern' age, typically dated between 1910 and 1930. In their now classic guide, Bradbury and McFarlane describe modernism as 'an art of a rapidly modernizing world, a world of rapid industrial development, advanced technology, urbanization, secularization and mass forms of social life', but also 'the art of a world from which many traditional certainties had departed, and a certain sort of Victorian confidence not only in the onward progress of mankind but in the very solidity and visibility of reality itself has evaporated' (Bradbury and McFarlane, 1976: 57). This double condition results in a central contradiction: depending on context and perspective, modernism can be seen as a vigorous creative impulse to 'make it new', through a determined break with the stultifying artistic conventions of the immediate past and an embrace of the modern, or as a literature of crisis and dislocation, desperately insisting on the power of art to give shape to a world that has lost all order and stability. Because modernism connotes a cultural sensibility rather than a particular period in time, however, it is not simply interchangeable with strictly historical references such as 'the early twentieth century' or 'the 1920s', even though it overlaps with them. The label 'high modernism' refers specifically to the canonical account of Anglo-American literary experimentation between the world wars, characterised by a turn away from direct modes of representation towards greater abstraction and aesthetic impersonality and self-reflexivity. Such aesthetic formalism is typically identified with the canonical figures of Ezra Pound and T. S. Eliot, as well as Joyce and Woolf. As a result of the insights of post-structuralist, feminist and post-colonial critics, however, the concept of modernism is now widely recognised to be open to much broader interpretation and redefinition than this reading previously acknowledged. See Bradbury and McFarlane, 1976; Faulkner, 1977; Levenson, 1984 and 1999; Eysteinsson, 1990; Kime Scott, 1990 and 1995; Nicholls, 1995; Goldman, 2004.

avant-garde in the 1910s, 1920s and 1930s, and encourage you to think critically about not only the possibilities but also the problems that Joyce, Woolf and Richardson's broadening of the scope of the novel posed for the burgeoning narrative of literary modernism.

What is immediately striking about the history of the modernist novel (and modernist fiction more generally) is the degree of its self-reflexivity, and in particular its theorising about its own 'newness'. Woolf, for example, was as notable as a professional literary critic in her lifetime as she was a novelist, and wrote widely on her own processes of writing and reading. She had begun in 1904, under the name of Virginia Stephen (she married Leonard Woolf in 1912), writing light essays for the clerical weekly *Guardian*, and biographical reviews for the *Cornhill Magazine*, where her father Sir Leslie Stephen had been an editor. Her main association, however, soon became with the *Times Literary Supplement*, to which she would contribute over one hundred anonymous review-essays. Increasingly frustrated by the constraints placed upon the free expression of her opinions by the editor Bruce Richmond, she also began to write for other major literary journals and magazines, notably the *Nation and Athenaeum*. The range of material that she dealt with across these pieces, from the Elizabethan period to the present day, provided the foundation for her revisionary thinking on literary history and essay-writing, and many were subsequently revised for *The Common Reader*, the two volumes of essays on the processes of reading, writing and criticism that were published by the Woolfs' Hogarth Press in 1925 and 1932. Her prodigious published output was further supplemented by a constant consideration of literary subject and form in her letters, notebooks and diaries. A further series of essay collections were put together by Leonard Woolf after her death (*The Death of the Moth* in 1942, *The Moment and Other Essays* in 1947, *The Captain's Death Bed* in 1950 and *Granite and Rainbow* in 1958).

Of course Woolf the novelist far outweighs Woolf the critic in literary renown, and until recently little attention had been paid to her non-fiction other than the oft-cited but rarely fully contextualised 'Modern Fiction' and 'Mr Bennett and Mrs Brown' essays as manifestos for the modernist novel, or of *A Room of One's Own* as a manifesto for twentieth-century literary feminism. This has changed with the publication of new and comprehensive editions of her essays edited by Andrew McNeillie (1986) and Rachel Bowlby (1992a; 1992b), and the subsequent rise of critical studies focussed on the implications of the essays for Woolf's canonical literary identity (Rosenberg, 1995; Brosnan, 1997; Dusinberre, 1997; Rosenberg and Dubino, 1997; Gualtieri, 2000). Woolf's essayistic practice, supplemented by the extensive consideration of the processes of reading and writing contained in her letters, notebooks and diaries, is now recognised as part of rather than subsidiary to her dominant concern with the expression of modern consciousness and the form of modern writing, evincing a strategic refusing of generic limits in which her conceptions of fiction and criticism, the novel and poetry, history and auto/ biography all come to resemble each other significantly.

Beginning to write reviews and essays at exactly the same time as Woolf (1904–5), but on a secretary's salary of little more than £1 per week, Dorothy Richardson exemplifies Woolf's argument in *A Room of One's Own* that writing could provide a means to female independence. 'Translations and freelance journalism had promised release from routine work that could not engage the essential forces of my being', she said of the moment when she decided to earn her living as a writer, '[t]he small writing-table in my attic became the centre of my life' (*JP*: 139). Richardson was not as prolific a critic as Woolf, and wrote on a diverse range of topics (from feminism, spiritualism and socialism, to literature and the cinema, to vegetarianism and dental health) in order to receive a minor yet regular income to support her fictional work. Her theories of writing and reading are yet in many ways interestingly comparable, from the discussions of gendered discourse and 'feminine' reality in 'Women and the Future' (1924), 'Women in the Arts' (1925), her regular column for the avant-garde film journal *Close-Up* (1927–32), and her foreword to the omnibus *Pilgrimage* in 1938, to her conception of the relationship of the modern writer and his/her ideal reader put forward in 'About Punctuation' (1924) and 'Adventure for Readers' (1939), a review of Joyce's *Finnegans Wake*. Finally available to current modernist scholars (Kime Scott, 1990; Friedberg, Marcus and Donald, 2001), these critical writings illuminate the feminist politics and aesthetics of *Pilgrimage*, her thirteen-volume life's work and twenty-year-long challenge to the masculine definition of the realist *and* modernist novel.

James Joyce is unusual in being a major 'modernist' who did not write extensively on modernist aesthetics, the financial patronage of Harriet Shaw Weaver from 1917 allowing him to devote himself entirely to his creative art. A number of essays written when he was a student at University College Dublin have been read retrospectively as anticipating thematic and formal concerns elaborated and then either discarded or evolved in his later fiction, notably 'Drama and Life', his paper defending the work of the Norwegian dramatist Henrik Ibsen, and 'The Day of the Rabblement' (1901), written for the college magazine, an attack on the parochialism of contemporary Irish theatre and the Irish cultural scene. Both polemical and highly divisive arguments in which Joyce separated himself from Catholic and nationalist opinion, they were initially suppressed by the college authorities, encouraging the precocious young student's cultivated stance of disdainful intellectual isolationism within what was actually a far more receptive and forward-thinking cultural scene than his subsequent reputation as Ireland's most famous prodigal son might suggest. By contrast the differences between Joyce's 1902 essay on the nineteenth-century Irish poet James Clarence Mangan and the revised version he gave as a lecture at the Università Popolare in Trieste in 1907, along with the two further lectures given as 'Realism and Idealism in English Literature', on Daniel Defoe and William Blake, signal his maturing artistic position away from the earlier attractions of abstract aestheticism towards a modern realism in which artistic vision combines with a considerable and not unsympathetic earthiness.

The fact that Joyce, Woolf and Richardson all saw themselves predominantly as novelists is yet an important proviso when considering them as 'critical thinkers'. Woolf, for example, warned strongly against any assumption that her critical writings offered evidence of her own aims in fiction, declaring that 'a novel is an impression not an argument' (*LVW* V: 91). It is an evasive but nevertheless legitimate caution. In considering Joyce, Woolf and Richardson's critical thinking on issues of literary form, history and aesthetics, we should not seek to make their novels merely vehicles of that thinking. As both novelists and critics they were fundamentally resistant towards the systematising of rational thought. When Joyce voices aesthetic principles in his fiction it is usually with heavy irony. Dorothy Richardson regarded all aesthetic, religious, scientific and philosophical theorising as the manifestation of a masculine (not for her a positive attribute!) understanding of the world. Woolf meanwhile resolutely identified herself with what she termed 'the common reader', refusing to take an authoritative position in her literary reviews and essays and typically presenting herself as an amateur muddling her way through insignificant ideas and anecdotes. All three writers actively extended questions of literary history, aesthetic theory and artistic strategy across their critical and fictional writings. Each felt that the novel had reached a moment of crisis, its generic conventions out of date and irrelevant for the expression of the character and conditions of a new age; each shared a heightened awareness of the disjunction between social action or language and internal states of consciousness; and each was committed to the belief that art could reveal the 'truth' beneath our familiar assumptions about the look and feel of reality. Yet while their statements on the representation of the relation of art and life have often been taken as clear manifestos for modern fiction, ultimately they question more than they answer, no fixed paradigm or critical concept of the 'modernist novel' emerging directly from their work. Rather than espousing any single and homogenous theory of the novel, Joyce, Woolf and Richardson were committed to a constant exploration and renegotiation of modern fiction's limits and possibilities.

The following chapters track a roughly chronological trajectory through the patterns, developments and reworkings of that endeavour. We begin with the vigorous debate on the future of the novel in the new century, and the search for an alternative realism in all three writers' early work. The representation of the subjective consciousness of one or more characters with no external commentary is perhaps the most immediately distinguishing technique of the modernist novel, and in Chapter 2 we will examine the different inflections that each writer gave to it. Yet significant as this stylistic device is to the modernist novel, what Joyce, Richardson and Woolf were perhaps thematically and structurally most concerned with was how to grasp and communicate what endures beneath or across the evanescence of subjective experience. For all the flux and flow of a Leopold Bloom, Miriam Henderson or Clarissa Dalloway's 'stream-of-consciousness', all three writers believed fundamentally in an underlying rhythm and connectedness to modern life, even if only infrequently and momentarily glimpsed. Intrinsic to an under-standing of the modernist novel, and its preoccupation with the relation of lived reality and aesthetic form, is a self-imposed and self-justifying emphasis on creative, connective vision.

A self-reflexive attention to style and form is central to Joyce, Richardson and Woolf's critical thinking on the novel and has always been a key theme of modernist literary criticism. With the waning influence of the New Criticism that dominated literary study in the 1950s, however, and a renewed interest in social and historical contexts and influences, the multiple and conflicting ideologies of modernist thought and modernist texts are being increasingly explored. As Bonnie Kime Scott observed of modernism in her landmark feminist study *The Gender of Modernism* in 1990, 'the making, the formal experiment, no longer seems to suffice as a definition. Mind, body, sexuality, family, reality, culture, religion, and his-tory were all reconstrued' (1990: 16). As we shall see Joyce, Richardson and Woolf's fictional works and critical writings constantly assert the *inseparability* of form and content, their rejection of the traditional forms and themes of art reflecting their various frustrations with and negotia-tions of a politicised and gendered social order. Woolf, for example, is as well known as a pioneer of feminist literary criticism as of the modernist novel, while Richardson's rejection of the gendered conventions of realist representation draws attention to and problematises modernism's own traditionally exclusive, classicist and gendered canon. Chapter 3 explores the representation of a specifically female consciousness in Woolf, Richardson and Joyce's writing as well as the identification of a feminine or androgynous aesthetic with avant-garde literary techniques more gen-erally. In Chapter 4, we will turn to the problem of history and nation-hood as it is considered across their work, from the haunting rupture of the First World War that was integral to the cultural identity and imagina-tion of the modernist novel in the 1920s, to the effort to recover the con-tinuity of past, present and future that marks its evolution in the 1930s.

Although outstandingly fertile, the 'modernist' moment was relatively short-lived. For a majority of writers from the later 1930s, the aesthetic experimentalism that had characterised the literature of the inter-war years was impossible to reconcile with the stance of social and political responsibility that the turmoil of a second world war and its aftermath

seemed to demand. By the 1940s a backlash against what was now perceived as the elitist and insular perspective of the modernist novel had re-
established the pre-eminence of a socially concerned realism. The legacy
of its self-reflexivity and experimentalism could not be disregarded, however, and subsequent writers ignored it at the risk of being declared aesthetically naïve and culturally parochial. A final chapter summarises the
main trends in subsequent literary criticism, highlighting some of the
ways in which the reception and impact of Joyce, Woolf and Richardson's
work has altered in accordance with the differing interests and purposes
of later historical and ideological contexts, from the anti-aestheticism of
the mid-twentieth century, to the cultural revisionings of the 1970s and
1980s, and the 'new' modernist studies of the present moment. This
guide should act as a stimulus to the current student's own participation
within this ever-continuing critical and common readership, the key ideas
it highlights not taken as prescriptive 'givens' to be rehearsed and regur-
gitated, but points of entry through which to begin to explore the modernist novel in all its demanding complexity, exhilarating inventiveness
and bewildering, unsettling yet revealing vision.

KEY IDEAS

1

A NEW REALISM

Intrinsic to an understanding of the modernist novel is its preoccupation with the relation of lived reality and aesthetic form. '[W]hat is reality? And who are the judges of reality?', Virginia Woolf asked in an essay on 'Character in Fiction' published in the literary journal *Criterion* in 1924 (*E* III: 426). 'Is life like this? Must novels be like this?', she demanded again the following year in 'Modern Fiction' (*E* IV:). 'Have I the power of creating the true reality?', she asked herself in her diary (*D* II: 248). Woolf was participating within a vigorous debate on the future of the novel in the new century, in which the appropriate form and focus of 'modern' fiction was yet by no means agreed. For despite a general consensus on all sides that the task of the novelist was the representation of 'reality', views on what actually constituted that reality, and on the most appropriate means for rendering it in fiction, were far more divergent. This chapter introduces Joyce and Richardson's development of a new 'psychological' realism, and Woolf's critical analysis of both its possibilities and its limits, within the context of this contested moment in the history of the modernist novel.

REALISM AND REALITY

From the very start of its relatively recent history the purpose of the English novel has arguably been the representation of everyday life – as opposed to the classical epic's focus on the heroic, for example, or the lyric's on private emotion. Theoretical accounts typically identify three main stages in the form of this representation through the novel's development as a major genre: a 'realist' model established in the eighteenth century, in which narrative is held to be capable of providing a direct imitation or equivalent of life, challenged by a 'modernist' psychological and linguistic self-consciousness about that imitation in the early twentieth, and a 'postmodernist' demystification of any straightforward correspondence between art and life from the 1960s.

Although influential, one problem with the theoretical delineation of the novel genre into the three key narrative stages highlighted above – realist, modernist and postmodernist – is that it encourages the homogenisation of what were historically far more contested positions of literary principle and narrative strategy. Eighteenth-century writers such as Daniel Defoe, Henry Fielding and Samuel Richardson pursued the 'reality effect' in clearly varying ways, while George Eliot, often described as an archetypal realist, was far from naïve in her self-conscious awareness of the *art* of representation. As Terry Eagleton observes in his recent history of the novel genre, however, '[t]o call something "realist" is to confess that it is not the real thing' (Eagleton, 2005: 10). The essential paradox of realism is that this is to undermine its central principle of seeming true to life. A writer's (or more broadly period's) ideological and epistemological position on the nature of reality will generally determine the narrative approach they take. While an eighteenth- or nineteenth-century novelist might acknowledge problems of subjective perspective and literary artifice, for example, they rarely allow them to intrude in such a way as to question the universal validity of the social, economic and moral scene presented (Lawrence Sterne is a notable exception). A contemporary 'postmodern' novelist, on the other hand, might regularly call attention to the fictionality of the world and characters he creates. Both, however, ultimately collapse life and artifice, towards one extreme or the other. We might think of the modern novelist as lying between these two poles, aiming to render in fiction the plurality and relativity of life as we experience it, at the same time as drawing attention to the creative effort of their art.

The origins of a 'new' realism can be found in the influence of Henry James (1843–1916). 'A novel is in its broadest definition a personal, a

REALISM

Literary realism in its most basic sense aims to provide a faithful representation of experiential reality. A common argument connects the origins of both realism and the novel with the development of liberal capitalism in the eighteenth century, and the secular, empirical and materialist understanding of the world it promoted (Watt, 1957; Bergonzi, 1970; Eagleton, 2005). Ian Watt, for example, defines the classic realist novel as based in 'the premise, or primary convention, that the novel is a full and accurate report of human experience' and 'therefore under an obligation to satisfy its reader with such details of the story as the individuality of the actors concerned, the particulars of the times and places of their actions, details which are presented through a more largely referential use of language than is common in other literary forms' (Watt, 1957: 32). The realist novel confidently assumes its ability to objectively convey to the reader an accurate imitation in verbal form of the kinds of details that Watt describes. Literary realism in this narrow sense is often contrasted with the formal experimentalism and internal, subjective focus of the modernist novel. According to this reading, and depending on the viewpoint of the critic, the realist novel presents either a reflection of the empirical world (a 'window onto reality') that is naïve and conservative in its failure to recognise the role of language and ideology in determining its perspective (Heath, 1972; Belsey, 1980), or a humanist engagement with the social world that is anti-elitist and politically progressive (Lodge, 1977). An important proviso when analysing the novel genre is to recognise that literary realism is an expansive and diverse concept, the understanding of 'reality' and the methods used to represent it altering according to time and circumstance. For an understanding of the complexity of realism and the nuanced debate over its definition, see Auerbach, 1953; Booth, 1961; Levine, 1981; Furst, 1992; Gasiorek, 1995; Herman, 1996; Morris, 2003.

direct impression of life: that, to begin with, constitutes its value', James had asserted in his essay 'The Art of Fiction' in 1884 (1956: 9). 'It goes without saying that you will not write a good novel unless you possess the sense of reality,' he continued, 'but it will be difficult to give you a recipe for calling that sense into being. Humanity is immense, and reality has a myriad forms' (12). While the representation of reality remained paramount within James' theory of the novel, his argument was yet that this could only be achieved through careful attention to artistic technique. James wanted to raise the status of the novel by encouraging a more theoretical understanding of its technical craft. '[I]t must take itself seriously for the public to take it so', he declared, and to do it needed 'a theory, a conviction, a consciousness of itself behind it' (44–5). James himself elaborated such a theory in the retrospective prefaces to his own novels that he wrote between 1907 and 1912, emphasising the importance of the writer's artistry in giving shape and greater illumination to the material of life.

The novels that James wrote in the 1900s, however, in which his method of concentrating the narrative through the limited perspective of one character's consciousness is most overt, appeared to mystify the reading public. The best-selling novels of the day were instead those of younger writers: H. G. Wells (1866–1946), Arnold Bennett (1867–1931) and John Galsworthy (1867–1933). They too believed it was the duty of the novelist to respond to changed times, and saw themselves as modernising a literary genre in which James was the establishment figure. The way in which they did so, however, was to emphasise not the impressionistic life of the individual but rather the social and material conditions of modern society at large. Wells, for example, presenting his own manifesto for the modern novel in a speech to the Times Book Club in 1911 (published in the *Fortnightly Review* later in the year as 'The Contemporary Novel'), argued that it was the duty of the novelist not to narrow his subject-matter to a concentration on the sensitivities of the human mind, but to engage in the social, moral and political problems of his time, and to use the novel as an instrument for this purpose. 'We are going to write about it all', he announced:

> We are going to write about business and finance and politics and precedence and pretentiousness and decorum and indecorum, until a thousand pretences and ten thousand impostures shrivel in the cold, clear air of our elucidations . . . Before we have done, we will have all life within the scope of the novel.
> (Parrinder and Philmus, 1980: 203)

As far as James was concerned, little could be further from *all* life than business and finance. In turn his own article on 'The New Novel' (1914) singled out Bennett and Wells as overloading their writing with material detail and description at the expense of imaginative perception. In so doing they only performed half the role of the novelist, he charged, presenting the raw matter of life without endowing it with the shape and form of art, and as a result never quite capturing the very reality they aimed at. Joseph Conrad put the same point somewhat more succinctly in a letter to Bennett in 1902, observing 'You just stop short of being absolutely real because you are faithful to your dogmas of realism' (Conrad, 1986: 390).

Wells responded angrily to James' criticism with a harsh parody of his one-time mentor as an out-dated aesthete in *Boon* (1915). The letter that James sent in reply contained a heartfelt reassertion of his aesthetic credo:

> so far from [the art] of literature being irrelevant to the literary report upon life . . .
> I regard it as relevant in a degree that leaves everything else behind. It is art that
> *makes* life, makes interest, makes importance, . . . and I know of no substitute
> whatever for the force and beauty of its process. (James, 1984: 770)

Essentially the two writers' understandings of the function of the novel and the nature of reality were deeply at odds. For Wells the novel was a means towards revolutionising society, and should convey its political commitment as straightforwardly and as explicitly as possible. For James it was an art form, which in skilful hands could enrich awareness of human experience. The debate over the means and purpose of a modern realism would be repeated in similar confrontations between Wells and Richardson, Bennett and Woolf, and Galsworthy and D. H. Lawrence. For despite Wells' confidence that it was the social arena that would inspire the modern novelist, the immediate future of the novel bore instead the mark of a Jamesian attention to the balance of artistry and reality in the capturing of conscious experience. James' insistence on the essential relationship of form and subject-matter, and his demand that the novel have 'a consciousness of itself', had set an aesthetic standard for a younger generation of writers seeking some kind of reference point in a changing social and artistic world. James 'is much at present in the air', Woolf wrote in 1918, 'a portentous figure looming large and undefined in the consciousness of writers, to some an oppression, to others an obsession, but undeniably present to all' (*E* I: 346).

ROMANTICISM, REALISM AND IMPRESSIONISM

At the same time as Wells was pursuing his disagreement with James in both public print and private correspondence, he was encouraging Dorothy Richardson to write a novel based on her own life as a young woman struggling for independence amidst the social, cultural and political scene of turn-of-the-century London. Wells appears in *Pilgrimage* as the novelist Hypo Wilson, with whom Miriam Henderson has a long relationship (a thinly veiled account of Richardson's own with Wells), as much literary apprenticeship as emotional entanglement. In *Clear Horizon*, when Wilson urges Miriam to write, it is something in his own style of socialist realism that he recommends: 'You have in your hands material for a novel, a dental novel, a human novel and, as to background, a complete period, a period of unprecedented expansion in all sorts of directions . . . You ought to document your period' (*P* IV: 397). While it is Wilson who praises and motivates Miriam's creative development, however, it is in resisting domination by his irrepressible self-belief that she is driven to express passionately and assert her own mind. Richardson herself had spent over a decade in intellectual dispute with H. G. Wells by the time she began to write *Pilgrimage*, and she shaped her novel more against than in accordance with his influence.

Richardson's opinion of Wells' fictional aesthetic is revealed in an early review, written for the magazine *Crank* in 1906, of his recent novel *In the Days of the Comet*. Following a career of analysing the 'here' and 'there' of external life, she notes,

> [t]here is, in this new book, an emotional deepening, a growth of insight and sympathy . . . for the first time that indefinable quality that fine literature always yields, that sense of a vast something behind the delicate fabric of what is articulated – a portentous silent reality. (Kime Scott, 1990: 400)

While commending this new recognition of an 'underlying reality' on Wells' part, however, Richardson ultimately critiques as much as she admires. His novels are full of too much 'stage machinery', she argues, novelistic conventions that obstruct the direct expression of his material to his readers. Moreover he cannot portray women, who are transformed across his work into the same 'rather irritating dummy', from the outside 'dressed up in varying trappings, with different shades of hair and proportions of freckles', but with no internal identity of their own. 'One hopes for a book where womanhood shall be as well as manhood', she declares (400). It was a novel of 'womanhood' that she herself was already in the process of planning to write. Her aim, as she recalled in her foreword to the collected edition of *Pilgrimage* in 1938, was to find 'a feminine equivalent' to the 'current masculine realism', clearly associated with the best-selling Wells, that she saw as dominating the first decade of the twentieth century (430).

While Richardson's retrospective 'Foreword' is regularly quoted in studies of her work, it promises a manifesto of her new 'feminine' realism that it never quite delivers. It had been requested by her publisher J. M. Dent in order to act as an introduction to the collected edition, but Richardson struggled with writing it, declaring it 'the most horrible job I ever attempted' (*LDR*: 341). The final piece is defensive and more than a little bitter in its comparison of her own obscurity to the recognised achievements of Joyce, Woolf and Marcel Proust, with whom she had been regularly compared in the 1910s and 1920s. It does, however, indicate Richardson's view of the history of literary realism, and the place of her own writing within it, that is more complex than a quick reading might initially suggest. The end of Romanticism is signified by the reference to the French writer Honoré de Balzac (1799–1850), who Richardson describes as the 'father of realism' (429) and whose long series of over ninety novels and stories on bourgeois life in post-Revolution France, *La Comédie humaine* (The Human Comedy), put an end to the previous hegemony of the gothic or historical novel in fiction. Balzac, along with Arnold Bennett, whom Richardson cites as the model of an equivalent realism in the English novel, focussed the novel on the observation of human society and psychology rather than imaginary or past worlds, in so doing turning the attention 'of the human spirit upon itself' (429). Yet while Balzac and Bennett pursued this focus on human nature instinctively, their successors at the beginning of the twentieth century took it up as a defining principle, substituting 'mirrors of plain glass' for the 'rose-coloured and distorting' lens of Romanticism, in what they thought to be a direct and documentary representation of reality (429). By 1911, however, Richardson asserts (and here she is recalling Wells' lecture on 'The Contemporary Novel'), the novel could be seen as distorting reality the other way, focussed almost entirely on 'explicit satire and protest' in order to promote the particular social or political cause of the author (429).

Looking for a model of the novel for her own work, Richardson states, she realised that all of these previous forms were dominated by men (she interestingly avoids all mention of George Eliot, although Miriam Henderson dismisses Eliot to Hypo Wilson as writing 'like a man'). With the only alternative being the Romantic-influenced women's novel (such as those of Charlotte Brontë, Ouida or Rosa Nouchette Cary that Miriam reads in *Pointed Roofs* and *Backwater*) she thus opted to attempt her own female version of this male realism. Initially she fails, setting aside 'a considerable mass of manuscript' with dissatisfaction because the form of this kind of novel seemed incompatible with her female experience of reality (430). 'The material that moved me to write would not fit the framework of any novel I had experienced', she later recalled, 'I believed myself to be, even when most enchanted, intolerant of the romantic and the realist novel alike. Each, so it seemed to me, left out certain essentials and dramatized life misleadingly' (*JP*: 139). If the type of 'feminine realism' that Richardson originally set out to write had been focussed in its *subject-matter* on female experience, she began to realise that to present such subject-matter would demand a different method of approach, that of 'contemplated reality having for the first time . . . its own say' (*P* 1: 431). It was this vision of 'independently assertive reality' (431) that led to the writing of *Pointed Roofs*. Ironically, after years of literary tutelage by Wells, it was an approach that she had glimpsed a decade before in the work of Henry James when, reading his novel *The Ambassadors* (1903), she had found herself fascinated by his technique of narrating the entire novel through the focus of a limited narrative point of view, 'the absence of direct narrative, of the handing out of information, descriptions of characters & so forth' (*LDR*: 595).

When Miriam Henderson reads *The Ambassadors* in book five of *Pilgrimage* (*The Trap*), she is thrilled at the 'unique power' of its opening

FREE INDIRECT DISCOURSE

Free indirect discourse is a technique for presenting a character's thoughts or speech without obvious mediation by an external narrator (Genette, 1980). It is distinct from direct speech (e.g. '"Look at those clouds. It might rain tomorrow", said Jane') and from indirect report ('Jane pointed to the clouds and warned that it might rain tomorrow'), in that it uses the third-person and past tense while moving inside the character's consciousness to take on the style and tone of their own immediate speaking voice ('The clouds looked dark and foreboding. It might rain tomorrow'). Because the use of the third-person retains an element of objective narration, free indirect discourse has been described as having a 'dual voice', able to convey at once the immediate thoughts of a character and the detached perspective of an impersonal narrator (Banfield, 1982). Jane Austen is credited with being the first English writer to make sustained use of free indirect discourse, an important technique for the development of the novel, although it is Henry James who is regarded as one of its greatest innovators, extending it to the point that his novels are focussed entirely through the non-omniscient perceiving consciousness of one central character. Subsequent theories of the novel, following James' influence, distinguished between modes of narrative that 'tell' (in which the author or authoritative narrator overtly directs the reader's interpretation of the characters and story) and those, like free indirect discourse, that 'show' (in which the author detaches his own point of view from the narrative, presenting scenes so that they tell themselves). The general consensus of those who made this argument was that 'showing' is superior to 'telling', and represents the *art* of fiction (Lubbock, 1921; Beach, 1932). Despite the difference between the neutrality of indirect narrative and the obvious value judgements of an overt authorial voice, however, there is arguably no straightforward distinction between 'showing' and 'telling'. The author always ultimately remains in control of the way narrative is represented, however much he ostensibly detaches himself from it.

pages, in which the reader learns only those aspects of plot and character available to the groping understanding of the central character Lambert Strether, declaring it 'the first completely satisfying way of writing a novel' (*P* III: 410). James' presentation of the novel through the prism of its central character suggested a way of avoiding the falsifying presence of an authorial narrator. 'I suddenly realized', Richardson recalled, 'that I couldn't go on in the usual way, telling *about* Miriam, describing her. There she was as I first saw her, going upstairs. But who was *there* to *describe* her? It came to me suddenly' (*JP*: 400). There was only Miriam, and what Richardson realised was of course that Miriam's description *of herself to herself* would be very different from that of an omniscient narrator external to the plot. Richardson was disillusioned, however, and Miriam like her, by James' portrait of the female character of Maria Gostrey, who through Strether's admiring gaze appears 'elaborately mysterious, allusive, indirect' (*LDR*: 595). We will examine Richardson's belief in the essential otherness of men and women, in mind, body and being, in Chapter 3. Here it will suffice to note that her aim in *Pilgrimage* was to fashion a form of narrative that would not only depict 'contemplated reality', but that would for the first time be true to the thoughts and impressions of a female point of view.

Pointed Roofs (1915), the first volume of *Pilgrimage*, opens with the seventeen-year-old Miriam Henderson launching herself nervously into independent life by taking a post (as Richardson had done over twenty years before) as a student teacher in Hanover. At first glance, Richardson's style seems conventional: 'Miriam left the gaslit hall and went slowly upstairs. The March twilight lay upon the landings, but the staircase was almost dark. The top landing was quite dark and silent. There was no one about. It would be quiet in her room' (*P* I: 15). As the reader proceeds, however, he realises that much of the information he has grown to expect from a novel and rely on is left out; about Miriam's appearance and age, her relationship with the various names mentioned, the why and where of her journey, etc. Scenes shift from one to another, and friends and acquaintances come and go, with little or no introduction or explanation. Instead of a stable vantage point from which to watch the unfolding of a narrative, he is instead placed within the mind of a young girl in the 1890s, subjected to her enthusiasms and anxieties, and restricted by the limits of her adolescent understanding. For Richardson's focus is not on the events of Miriam's life that would normally constitute plot (there are few, and readers of the subsequent volumes waited for a romantic denouement in vain), but on the ways in which she experiences that life. As the novelist May Sinclair (1863–1946) recognised, in a review of *Pointed Roofs*, *Backwater* and *Honeycomb* that appeared in the avant-garde literary journals *The Egoist* and the *Little Review* in April 1918, Richardson had evolved an extreme version of free indirect narrative technique in which:

> she must not interfere; she must not analyse or comment or explain. . . . she must not tell a story or handle a situation or set a scene; she must avoid drama as she avoids narration. . . . She must not be the wise, all-knowing author. She must be Miriam Henderson. She must not know or divine anything that Miriam does not know or divine; she must not see anything that Miriam does not know or see. (Kime Scott, 1990: 443)

It is this positioning of the narrative entirely and unceasingly within Miriam's consciousness that accounts for the lack of external information given to the reader. Miriam is not going to describe her surroundings or explain the context of her actions *to herself* because she is already familiar with them. Instead the reader, given access to her thoughts, reflections and impressions, is left to piece together the external action and scene through a process of deduction and cross-reference. As Richardson stated in 1923, 'Information there must be, but the moment it's given directly as information, the sense of immediate experience is gone' (*LDR*: 68).

As noted above, when Edward Garnett, the editor and reader for Duckworth, accepted *Pointed Roofs* for publication in 1915, he described the focus of the narrative on Miriam's perceiving consciousness as the first example of 'feminine impressionism' in literature (Fromm, 1977: 77). Over two decades later Ford Madox Ford would identify Richardson as the at once 'abominably unknown' yet 'most distinguished exponent' of impressionist realism in the early twentieth-century novel (Ford, 1947: 773). Richardson's method, he noted, concentrated on the 'minuteness of rendering of objects and situations perceived through the psychologies of the characters' (773). External details, always mediated through Miriam's perceptions, are used not for mimetic effect and the construction of a tangible reality, but as indicators of her various states of mind, her evolving opinions, and developing sense of selfhood in relation to her environment and those around her. Richardson herself would later state that it was only Ford who had ever understood what she was trying to do, the 'representation of life-as-experience' (*LDR*: 629) from a feminine point of view.

J. D. Beresford, writing the introduction to *Pointed Roofs*, was faced with the task of explaining Richardson's new method to what he suspected would be a somewhat bewildered reading audience. At first, he acknowledged, he had thought its method to be realist and objective, on a second reading felt it was the most subjective novel he had ever read, but finally decided that it was something altogether distinct from either of these categories, possessing 'a peculiar difference which is, perhaps, the mark of a new form in fiction' (Richardson, 1915: vii). While praising the novel he yet also felt the need to 'prepare the mind of the reader for something that he or she might fail otherwise properly to understand' (vi). He was right. A first review, in the *Sunday Observer*, was positive, praising the clarity of Richardson's style, which it said seemed to be written 'as if the reader did not exist' (Fromm, 1977: 79). Many conventional readers, however, faced with a novel with no obvious plot, no clear beginning or end, and in which the author rudely left out key events that propelled one scene to another, disliked being so disregarded. A notice in the *Saturday Review* described it as 'pages and upon pages of foolish or fevered fantasies' from a self-absorbed 'egoistic consciousness' (80). For a publication in which twenty fictional sketches by Richardson had

LITERARY IMPRESSIONISM

The concept of literary impressionism refers to an aesthetic principle and form of narrative technique typically associated with the writers Joseph Conrad and Ford Madox Ford. Derived from the empirical philosophy of David Hume (1711–76), and advocated by Ford as an extension or revision of realism, it was concerned with both representing the subjective perception of external stimuli by the individual mind, and encouraging the reader's own sensory participation in forming an impressionistic response to the text. Stylistically it is characterised by narrative devices that obscure facts and meaning, such as unreliable or equivocal narrators, or fragmented chronology. In 'On Impressionism' (1914), for example, Ford describes it as 'the record of the impression of a moment . . . not the correlated chronicle' (Ford, 2003: 267).

appeared between 1908 and 1914, the *Review* was strangely unsympathetic to her experimental novel. 'Miss Richardson is recognised as a writer whose method is original', drily acknowledges a review of *Backwater* in 1916, adding that 'In so far as that method of writing consists of writing telegraphese, and putting words by themselves with full stops after them, it is not to be commended. Nothing is to be gained by it equal to the handicaps which it imposes on the reader'.

That unusual layout and punctuation made *Pilgrimage* unreadable, became an increasingly common complaint among readers, who even if prepared to accept Richardson's unwavering focus on Miriam's point of view proved less tolerant of her experimentation with graphic style (Mepham, 2000). Miriam's internal monologue is typically given in long stretches of unparagraphed text, the punctuation and syntax of which flouts convention. Richardson leaves out full stops, allows sentences to remain unfinished, or switches between past and present tense or from third- to first-person narrative. Dialogue and reported speech, moreover, is set *within* the flow of Miriam's consciousness rather than on separate lines of text, so that the reader must follow carefully to work out who is speaking. Again, however, Richardson believed that she was following the requirements of her method. The rules of punctuation are only mechanical tools that help to make communication straightforward and easy, she argues in an essay 'About Punctuation' in an article in the *Adelphi* in 1924, but they dull our responses to the natural rhythm of prose and thus have 'devitalized the act of reading; have tended to make it less organic, more mechanical' (Kime Scott, 1990: 415). That her distinction between mechanical and organic prose is importantly gendered is made clear in the later 'Foreword'. 'Feminine prose', she states here, 'should properly be unpunctuated, moving from point to point without formal obstructions' (431). Her application of punctuation is irregular because it was unconscious, the result of a 'habit of ignoring, while writing, the lesser of the stereotyped system of signs' (431), and therefore closer to her natural expression.

Richardson extended this strategy to its most extreme in the two books that appeared in 1919, *The Tunnel* and *Interim*, which in following the beginning of Miriam's London life, the trauma of her mother's suicide and her self-immersion in the distractions of both work and leisure, register a change in the tone of her perceiving consciousness. Given that *Interim* also appeared in instalments in the *Little Review* in 1919, being serialised alongside *Ulysses*, Richardson perhaps reasonably expected that readers of such avant-garde writing would be receptive to her own innovations in linguistic and graphic style. She was disappointed. Few readers made any connection between Miriam's experiences and the changing style of her interior monologue, even those, like Woolf and Katherine Mansfield, who were themselves writers and regular reviewers of experimental prose (we will explore Woolf and Mansfield's response to Richardson's depiction of female consciousness in the following chapter). *Pilgrimage* never sold well at any point of its twenty-year publication history, but as early as the mid-1920s her English and American publishers were struggling to recoup their costs from poor sales. By the publication of the collected edition, for which the text of the original books was reset with more conventional speech marks, paragraphing and line breaks, she was admitting with defeat that her attempt to write 'feminine prose' had resulted in a textual 'chaos' for which she was 'justly reproached' (432). James Joyce, who in the final section of *Ulysses* would make a similar yet far more famous attempt, would suffer no such recrimination.

DRAMA AND LIFE

'I think there is a new phase in the works of Mr. Joyce', declared the American poet Ezra Pound in 1914, reviewing *Dubliners* (Deming, 1970). 'Mr. Joyce writes a clear hard prose', he continued, 'He deals with subjective things, but he presents them with such clarity of outline that he might be dealing with locomotives or with builders' specifications.' It is this emphasis on the *clarity* of Joyce's writing, which Pound would reiterate again and again over the next few years, that some of the early reviews of *Pilgrimage* echoed, the work of both novelists being drawn under the banner of Imagism's 'new' realism. We will see over the course of this book how Joyce, Woolf and Richardson's experiments in prose were consistently appropriated by critics in a manner that has often come subsequently to define the initial experiments themselves. Pound here is no exception, emphasising the Imagist precision of Joyce's 'realism' while downplaying those aspects that patently contradicted such formal control.

Joyce's supposed modernist formalism, as argued by Pound, is often supported by quotation from Stephen Daedalus' famous declaration of aesthetic impersonality at the end of *A Portrait of the Artist as a Young Man*, published later in the same year in *The Egoist*, at Pound's invitation. It is important not to take the novel as a straightforward articulation of Joyce's own aesthetic theories however. The novel is a gently satiric portrait of the artist as a *young* man, and is as revealing of attitudes that Joyce abandoned as much as aims he refined. Even as a student himself, Joyce had not subscribed to a belief in the severance of art and life in the way that the Stephen of *A Portrait of the Artist as a Young Man* seems to (and that the Stephen of *Ulysses* looks back on with ridicule). The views expressed in the paper 'Drama and Life' that he read to the University College Literary and Historical Society in 1900, for example, and for which he was accused of supporting the principle of art-for-art's sake, are at odds with any narrow aestheticist doctrine. For while refusing the demand that art should have an ethical aim, Joyce suggests that the aesthete's claim that beauty is the ultimate object of art is also false. The object of art is 'truth', and truth is often neither ethical nor beautiful (although art when it deals with truth becomes so). Indeed art is disfigured by the 'mistaken insistence on its religious, its moral, [*and*] its beautiful, its idealising tendencies' (*OCP*: 27), an attitude that denies the truth of modern times and harks back to the values of a previous age. The modern artist, Joyce claims, must depict life in all its dreary and vulgar reality, recognising the material of drama as it exists within the common world rather than creating it through the falsity of legend:

> Shall we put life – real life – on the stage? . . . I think out of the dreary sameness of existence, a measure of dramatic life may be drawn. Even the most commonplace, the deadest among the living, may play a part in a great drama. . . . Life we must accept as we see it before our eyes, men and women as we meet them in the real world, not as we apprehend them in the world of faery. The great human comedy in which each has share, gives limitless scope to the true artist, today as yesterday and as in years gone by. (28)

In arguing for the role of the commonplace in art here, Joyce is aligning himself with a European model of literary realism embodied by his twin heroes Gustave Flaubert (1821–80) and Henrik Ibsen (1828–1906), in which the objective depiction of mundane everyday life is combined with a refusal of moral accountability and a preoccupation with formal artistry and technique. It is the *formalism* of Flaubert and Ibsen (along with that of Henry James) that makes for their regular appropriation as predecessors of modern realism by many writers and critics in the 1910s and 1920s, including Joyce, Woolf and Richardson, in contrast to the more materialist realism they identified in the writing of their immediate predecessors such as H. G. Wells or Arnold Bennett. What Joyce in particular inherits from Flaubert, James and Ibsen in 'Drama and Life', is the principle that the seemingly trivial and minor incidents of individual, modern lives, when portrayed with perfect artistic concentration and arrangement, can reveal the broader essence of existence that is common to all. The true aim of literary drama, Joyce asserts, has always been the capturing of that essence or spirit of reality.

It is worth noting at this point that Joyce's focus on 'drama' should not be taken too literally. It predominates in his early writings largely due to the influence of Ibsen, but what he seems to have in mind is typically not theatrical drama as such but rather any art that might reveal what he describes as the 'underlying laws' (24) of existence. 'Human society', he declares, 'is the embodiment of changeless laws which the whimsicalities and circumstances of men and women involve and overwrap' (23). While literature, he suggests, and here he seems to mean a 'traditional' realism, specialises in the portrayal of those transient fashions and events, the proper subject of drama is what lies beneath:

> By drama I understand the interplay of passions to portray truth; drama is strife, evolution, movement in whatever way unfolded; it exists before it takes form, independently; it is conditioned but not controlled by its scene. It might be said fantastically that as soon as men and women began life in the world there was above them and about them, a spirit, of which they were dimly conscious . . . and for whose truth they became seekers in after times, longing to lay hands upon it. For this spirit is as the roaming air, little susceptible of change, and never left their vision, shall never leave it, till the firmament is as a scroll rolled away. (25)

Various art forms (the morality play, the mystery, the ballet, pantomime and opera) have tried to portray this spirit, and at present it is only 'the drama' (by which he does mean dramatic theatre) that has managed to succeed. This does not mean that no other mode of art could do so, however. Indeed Joyce seems to consider that in fact the appropriate *mode* of dramatic art will continuously alter, noting that '[a]t times it would seem that the spirit had taken up his abode in this or that form – but on a sudden he is misused, he is gone and the abode is left idle'. Drama might take many forms, and Joyce's demand is simply that '[w]hatever form it takes must not be superimposed or conventional' (25), must not begin to assume its codes of representation provide a fixed norm. Greek drama, for example, he describes as 'played out' (23). If literature could release itself from the shackles of convention, then there is nothing in Joyce's argument to deny that it too cannot become the dramatic art form of modern life. 'Drama will be for the future at war with convention, if it is to realise itself truly' (25), he declares, outlining an aesthetic creed that he himself would eventually push to its extreme in bringing together the two types of art that in this essay are fundamentally distinct: drama and literature.

Joyce began writing *Dubliners* in 1904, describing it as 'a series of epicleti', through which he aimed 'to betray the soul of that hemiplegia or paralysis which many consider a city' (*LJJ* I: 55). Portraying moments of brief (or failed) spiritual perception, or what Joyce referred to as an 'epiphany', occurring within otherwise trivial episodes from everyday life, these short pieces offer an early indication of Joyce's attempt to work through, in his own art, the argument in 'Drama and Life'.

At the same time as working on *Dubliners*, Joyce was attempting a more conventional literary account of his early artistic aspirations and flight from the insularity and sterility of Dublin life under the title *Stephen Hero*. The short sketches, however, would seem to have excited Joyce far more than his unwieldy autobiographical novel. 'I am afraid I cannot finish my novel for a long time', he wrote to his brother Stanislaus, 'I am discontented with a great deal of it and yet how is Stephen's nature to be expressed otherwise?' (Ellmann, 1982: 71). The answer was to be found in the bare realism of the shorter pieces, which Joyce declared were written 'in a style of scrupulous meanness and with the conviction that he is a

EPIPHANY

A product of the earnest youthful aestheticism that as a mature artist he soon came to mock, Joyce first used the term 'epiphany' to describe the notebook sketches of Dublin life that he wrote in the early 1900s. To his brother Stanislaus he declared that an epiphany revealed 'the significance of trivial things' (Ellmann, 1982: 169), endowing the most common object with value. At other times, however, the experience of epiphany is presented as stemming from the direct opposite, an abstract aesthetic revelation rather than a prosaic object or instance from everyday life. This ambiguity is epitomised in *Stephen Hero*, the early draft of *A Portrait of the Artist as a Young Man*, when Stephen eulogises: 'By an epiphany he meant a sudden spiritual manifestation, whether in *the vulgarity of speech or of gesture or in a memorable phase of the mind itself*. He believed that it was for the man of letters to record these epiphanies with great care, seeing that they themselves are the most delicate and evanescent of moments' [my italics]. Joyce jotted numerous such records in his notebooks between 1902 and 1904, to the annoyance of those friends and associates who found themselves the object of them. Thirteen of these reappeared in *Stephen Hero*, twelve in *A Portrait of the Artist as a Young Man* and four in *Ulysses*, although Stephen himself mocks the idea of the epiphany as an example of his earlier aesthetic pretensions. As an artistic technique the epiphany nevertheless retains significance for Joyce's own thinking on the novel; notably in its episodic nature, which forms the basic structure of *A Portrait*, *Ulysses* and *Finnegans Wake*, but also in the tension it reveals, and that would persist throughout Joyce's work, between the abstract and material origins of artistic creation.

very bold man who dares to alter in the presentment, still more to deform, whatever he has seen and heard' (*LJJ* II: 134).

In 1907 he started to rewrite *Stephen Hero* as *A Portrait of the Artist as a Young Man*. The revised version was radically different in method and style, restricting the narrative perspective to a quasi-autobiographical central protagonist instead of an all-seeing, all-knowing narrator. It was also far more concise, the amount of external events and scenes portrayed significantly reduced because nothing could be made available to the reader that was not experienced by Stephen himself. Interestingly, given the formal artistic control that we will see was subsequently attributed to Joyce's work, Edward Garnett, the same reader who accepted *Pointed Roofs* for publication with Duckworth, rejected *A Portrait* for being 'too discursive, formless, unrestrained' (Deming, 1970: 81). That it was 'unconventional' would not stand against it in the present literary climate, he admitted, but it needed 'time and trouble spent on it, to make it a more finished piece of work, to shape it more carefully as the product of the craftmanship, mind and imagination of an artist'. Of the final pages, in which the interior monologue of the quasi-autobiographical Stephen Dedalus is conveyed in diary form, he stated, 'the pieces of writing and the thoughts are all in pieces and they fall like damp, ineffective rockets' (Deming, 1970: 81).

The opening line of *A Portrait of the Artist as a Young Man* – 'Once upon a time and a very good time it was there was a moocow coming down along the road and this moocow that was coming down along the road met a nicens little boy named baby tuckoo. . . ' – announced this 'new style' to readers with brazen assurance (*PA*: 5). It also reveals one of the distinctive characteristics of his extension of literary realism. Richardson, as we have seen, attempts to register in words the impression of reality as it is perceived and recorded by the mind. Joyce does so too, but for him that impression is constituted by language in the first place, and influenced in different ways by different forms of discourse and rhetoric. It is this preoccupation that leads to the slippage (but also interdependence) of *language* and consciousness, and the parodying and pastiche of literary and cultural linguistic styles, in both *Ulysses* and *Finnegans Wake*. What makes the opening of *A Portrait of the Artist as a Young Man* so striking, for example, is that Joyce is presenting Stephen's internal narrative in accordance with infant idiom. As he grows older the style of the narrative similarly shifts to reflect the kinds of language he is exposed to (flowery and sentimental after his reading of romantic literature, for example, tortured and grotesque after Father Arnall's hell-and-damnation sermon, sensual and ecstatic with his developing aestheticism). There are few such fluctuations in the tone of Miriam's interior monologue (Virginia Woolf joked in a review of *Revolving Lights* in 1923 that if a man fell dead at Miriam's feet her attention would probably be caught by the precise shade of light that formed part of the experience; see *E* III: 365–8).

Joyce, however, does not relinquish the same degree of authorial control to a restricted point of view as Richardson does, and after the initial lines the majority of the novel is presented through the mediation of an increasingly ironic third-person narrator. It is because of the predominantly 'dual-voice' of Joyce's free indirect style that Stephen the university student, preaching his aesthetic theories to his fellow students, appears more self-opinionated and remote than in the diary entries of the final pages when the narrative switches to a more direct internal monologue. Compare for example the conversation between Stephen and Cranly over his refusal to attend Easter confession, which takes over ten pages in free indirect style, with the paragraph summary of it in Stephen's first-person diary. In the first, Stephen's self-important declaration of artistic independence, 'I will try to express myself in some mode of life or art as freely as I can and as wholly as I can, using for my defence the only arms I allow myself to use – silence, exile, and cunning', is undercut by Cranly's sympathetic but mocking response: 'Cunning indeed! he said. Is it you? You poor poet, you!' (*PA*: 208). In the second he records, 'Long talk with Cranly on the subject of my revolt. He had his grand manner on. I supple and suave' (*PA*: 209). Stephen's immature arrogance is still in evidence, but it is more immediate, and revealed by his own narrative rather than through interplay with another person. *Pilgrimage* lacks this ironic element, partly because Richardson is more sympathetic towards her alter-ego, but also because the narrative is strictly filtered throughout by the prism of Miriam's consciousness and the reader therefore is never given an external perspective from which to view the other 'characters' she comes into contact with.

Joyce regularly claimed that from *Dubliners* onward his work was constantly in development, 'always *in progress*' (Beja, 1992: 31), pushing the boundaries of artistic form to capture better the drama of life. The point of his own aesthetic development in the 1910s, from which he looks back at his younger self in *A Portrait of the Artist as a Young Man* with such ironic detachment, and the evolution of the ideas put forward in the earlier 'Drama and Life' essay, is interestingly suggested by a pair of lectures on 'Realism and Idealism in English Literature' (focussed, respectively, on Daniel Defoe and William Blake) that Joyce gave in Trieste in 1912. Across the two lectures Joyce again distinguishes between the relative realms and possibilities of the novelistic and the poetic imagination, but now in order to finally bring them together. In his description of Defoe, 'the father of the English novel', as the first writer 'to create without literary models, to instil a national spirit into the creations of his pen, and to manufacture an artistic form for himself that is perhaps without precedent' (*OCP*: 164), there is as much of a self-portrait as there is in the Ibsenite or Flaubertian Stephen of *A Portrait of the Artist as a Young Man*. Impersonal artistic method is here grounded in a statistical realism that is cinematic in its precision and shockingly indecent in its clarity. Defoe's literary method reaches its limits for Joyce, however, in its disregard of the spiritual side of man. This he finds in the work of Blake, whose mystic idealism opposes the prosaic, refuses the bounds of space and time, and allows him to move 'from the infinitely small to the infinitely big, from a drop of blood to the universe of stars' (182). In this emphasis on human perception *and* aesthetic form, the tragedies and comedies of everyday life *and* the archetypal laws of human existence, cinematic realism *and* creative correspondence, the artist as 'indefatigable scribbler' (166) *and* the artist as visionary genius, lay the germ of *Ulysses*.

MYTH AND THE MODERN

Following the thoughts and perceptions of first Stephen Dedalus and then Leopold Bloom through one day in Dublin, what most struck early readers of *Ulysses* was its encyclopaedic but prosaic realism. 'It is the realistic novel par excellence' (266), Pound declared, continuing that 'Ulysses is not a book that everybody is going to admire . . . but it is a book that every serious writer needs to read . . . in order to have a clear idea of the point of development of our art' (Deming, 1970: 266). Of course it is not a traditional realism that Pound has in mind here, but one in which the standard demand for a 'story' is removed, to be replaced instead by an emphasis on the exact presentation of life achieved through precise literary technique. For a majority of readers, however, faced with the 1922 text from which the original Homeric chapter headings attached to the *Little Review* instalments had been removed, the technique of the novel was overwhelmed by the sheer limitlessness of ever-increasing detail. The typical response was that of Arnold Bennett, who declared that he regarded *Ulysses* from two extremes: either bored by its 'pervading difficult dullness' (Deming, 1970: 219) or shocked to the point of dropping it. His combination of praise and censure, he admitted, was extravagant, but that, he concluded, 'is how I feel about James Joyce' (219).

The mythical structure of the novel, based on Homer's *Odyssey*, went relatively unrecognised until the lecture and accompanying essay (published in the prestigious *Nouvelle Revue Française* in April 1922) by the French writer Valery Larbaud. An astute and receptive critic, who had discussed *Ulysses* at length with Joyce himself, Larbaud elucidated its mythical and symbolic parallels:

> We begin to discover and to anticipate symbols, a design, a plan, in what appeared to us at first a brilliant but confused mass of notations, phrases, data, profound thoughts, fantasticalities, splendid images, absurdities, comic or dramatic situations; and we realise that we are before a much more complicated book than we had supposed, that everything which appeared arbitrary and sometimes extravagant is really deliberated and premeditated; in short that we are before a book which has a key.

This 'key' is the *Odyssey*, the eighteen 'chapters' of the novel structured in correspondence with the adventures of Ulysses on his return from the battle of Troy. The clearest Homeric parallels soon become apparent to the careful reader, Larbaud optimistically asserted, who will note the transposition of Bloom's episodic 'journey' onto the streets and locations of early twentieth-century Dublin, and across the hours of one day. His exposition of the full intricacies of Joyce's structural method, however, depended on Joyce's now infamous schema (published by Stuart Gilbert in his *James Joyce's Ulysses* in 1931), in which each episode is titled according to a corresponding event or character from the *Odyssey*, but also meticulously assigned a series of correspondences: a scenic setting, hour of the day, bodily organ, art or philosophy, colour, symbol and mode of narration. Joyce explained: 'Each adventure (that is, every hour, every organ, every art being interconnected and interrelated in the structural scheme of the whole) should not only condition but even create its own technique'. The schema has undoubtedly proved the most significant example of Joyce's wily and mischievous spin-doctoring of his literary reputation, but he later regretted the emphasis on the virtuosity of the technics of the novel that it encouraged. Nevertheless, it does help to elucidate the panoply of literary styles and metaphors, far more radical than in *A Portrait of the Artist as a Young Man*, through which the particular subject and tone of each episode is presented; from the strident headlines of 'Aeolus', for example, to the mimicking of the rhythms and arrangements of musical form and tone in 'Sirens', bigoted nationalist rhetoric in 'Cyclops', the magazine romance that shapes the thoughts of the adolescent Gerty MacDowell in 'Nausicaa', the history of English prose in 'Oxen of the Sun', the carnivalesque performance of 'Circe', or the flowing prose of the female body in 'Penelope'. For Joyce, far from an over-emphasis on technical artifice, these different stylistic modes were entirely in accordance with his attempt to represent modern life. When asked, for example, whether literature should be a record of fact or the creation of art, he reportedly replied, 'It should be life' (Power, 1999: 43). He continued, however, 'in my opinion there are as many forms of art as there are forms of life' (45).

The publication of *Ulysses*, T. S. Eliot announced in his essay 'Ulysses, Order and Myth' in 1923, rendered the novel genre obsolescent. If it did not seem to conform to what was expected of a novel, he argued, that was because the form of the novel was of no use to modern literature, 'because the novel, instead of being a form, was simply the expression of an age which had not sufficiently lost all form to feel the need of something stricter' (Faulkner, 1986: 103). The modern age, he implied, did need something stricter, something that perhaps could be found in the elaborate design of epic form, as demonstrated by the use of the *Odyssey* as the structural model for *Ulysses*. 'In using the myth,' he continued,

> in manipulating a continuous parallel between contemporaneity and antiquity, Mr. Joyce is pursuing a method which others must pursue after him. They will not be imitators, any more than the scientist who uses the discoveries of an Einstein in pursuing his own, independent, further investigations. It is simply a way of controlling, of ordering, of giving a shape and a significance to the immense panorama of futility and anarchy which is contemporary history. . . . Instead of narrative method, we may now use the mythical method. It is, I seriously believe, a step toward making the modern world possible for art. (103)

Eliot was defending Joyce from the common charge among early readers that his talent, while extraordinary, was nevertheless 'undisciplined', and that *Ulysses* was in its style 'an invitation to chaos' and in its subject 'an expression of feelings which are perverse, partial, and a distortion of reality' (101); the very kind of reading that was also regularly applied to Richardson's *Pilgrimage*. While more applicable to Eliot's own work than to *Ulysses*, it has become one of the most influential accounts of 'high modernism'; the drive to impose a universal and eternal artistic shape on the manifold chaos of modernity. Yet it also served to divert attention from the *disruptive* impulse that pervades Joyce's oeuvre, in a manner that had significant repercussions on the reception of the modernist novel. The sprawling wordiness and unrefined 'realism' by which early reviewers, including Ezra Pound, had initially defined Joyce's work, is 'disciplined' as it were, by Eliot's critical pen. *Ulysses* in Eliot's eyes is a model of artistic control, its systematic method comparable to that of science. It is, significantly, not a 'novel' (which Eliot implies are loose, strict messy things) at all, but instead an 'epic'. It is not written as 'narrative' but as 'myth'. It does not so much communicate the reality of modern life as restrain it. The more unruly aspects of the novel – the teeming mass of detail that makes up the social, spatial and cultural life of Dublin in 1904, and the shock, awe, repulsion, hilarity and even boredom that this evoked (and continues to evoke) in its readers – are subdued in Eliot's account by the weightiness of an abstract European literary tradition.

Joyce's own comments on classical and modern literary form suggest that he agreed with Eliot's emphasis on the order of the former and chaos of the latter, but diverged significantly from Eliot's argument that the one should be used to control the other. Classical literature, he said in conversation with Arthur Power, concerned itself with action and the physical world, in accordance with the mindset of its time. It was yet incapable of expressing the subjective world that he regarded as central within the experience of modern life:

> When it has to deal with motives, the secret currents of life which govern everything, it has not the orchestra, for life is a complicated problem. It is no doubt flattering and pleasant to have it presented in an uncomplicated fashion, as the classicists pretend to do, but it is an intellectual approach which no longer satis-

fies the modern mind, which is interested above all in subtleties, equivocations and the subterranean complexities which dominate the average man and compose his life. I would say that the difference between classical literature and modern literature is the difference between the objective and the subjective: classical literature represents the daylight of the human personality while modern literature is concerned with the twilight, the passive rather the active mind. (Power, 1999: 85)

Joyce, while acknowledging that the writer 'must take both worlds into consideration' and commending Eliot for having done so himself to clever effect in his poem *The Waste Land* (1922), asserted that it was 'the hidden or subconscious world' of the modern that he found 'the most exciting' (87). Ibsen, he argued, was a writer whose 'brilliant research into modern life' had explored 'new psychological depths which have influenced a whole generation' (42, 43). His own work attempted to do something similar for his own modern moment. No other writer, he declared, had 'taken modern psychology so far, or to such a fine point' (90) as he had done in writing *Ulysses*:

I have opened the new way . . . In fact, from it you may date a new orientation in literature – the new realism; . . . a new way of thinking and writing has been started, and those who don't fall in with it are going to be left behind. Previously writers were interested in externals . . . they thought only on one plane, but the modern theme is the subterranean forces, those hidden tides which govern everything and run humanity counter to the apparent flood. (64)

Rather than the destruction of the novel, Joyce here asserts again a 'new realism' which breaks with objective, externalising narrative convention in order to reveal the subjective experience of life. Significantly, however, he emphasises not so much the conscious impressions of the mind as Richardson was doing, but the deeper, more unruly forces of essential existence that Eliot suggests in *Ulysses* he sets out to control:

Our object is to create a new fusion between the exterior world and our contemporary selves, and also to enlarge our vocabulary of the subconscious as Proust has done. We believe that it is in the abnormal that we approach closer

to reality. When we are living a normal life we are living a conventional one, following a pattern which has been laid out by other people in another generation,
an objective pattern imposed upon us by the church and state. But a writer
must maintain a continual struggle against the objective: that is his function. The
eternal qualities are the imagination and the sexual instinct, and the formal life
tries to suppress both. (86)

'[I]n writing one must create an endlessly changing surface, dictated by
the mood and current impulse in contrast to the fixed mood of classical
style', Joyce commented, '[t]his is "Work in Progress". The important
thing is not what we write, but how we write, and in my opinion the
modern writer must be an adventurer above all, willing to take every
risk, and be prepared to founder in his effort if need be' (109–10). His
own *Work in Progress*, begun after the publication of *Ulysses* and finished,
finally, as *Finnegans Wake* in 1938, continued that adventure through the
subterranean complexities of the modern mind: 'Since 1922, when I
began *Work in Progress*, I haven't really lived a normal life', he later
declared, '[s]ince 1922 my book has been a greater reality for me than
reality' (Ellmann, 1982: 695).

MODERN NOVELS

While Joyce and Richardson arguably pioneered the new psychological
realism, it is Virginia Woolf's formulation of this focus and technique in
her essay 'Modern Novels' (1919) and its revised version 'Modern
Fiction' (1925) that has most influenced subsequent summaries of modernist fictional method. Often read as a manifesto for Woolf's own aesthetic objectives, 'Modern Fiction' is in fact largely a critique of the
methods of her contemporaries, and reveals the ambiguities and variations
within the emerging literary aesthetics of the 1910s and 1920s, rather
than advocating any particular definition or literary method appropriate
to the modern novel.

Woolf had read both Richardson and Joyce immediately before writing
the 'Modern Novels' essay, having reviewed the fourth book of *Pilgrimage*,
The Tunnel, for the *TLS* in February. In 1923, moreover, she reviewed the
seventh book, *Revolving Lights*, and was clearly impressed with

Richardson's method, crediting her with inventing a 'psychological sentence of the feminine gender' (*E* III: 367). Her final decision to leave any mention of Richardson and the method of *Pilgrimage* out of both the 1919 essay and its revised version in 1925 is therefore surprising. Given the subsequent influence of the essay in canonical accounts of the modernist novel, it has also had the effect of obscuring Richardson's own role within the development of the modern novel.

The central argument of 'Modern Fiction' is based in a contrast between the 'materialist' narrative focus of Wells, Bennett and Galsworthy and the new 'spiritualist' focus of the 'moderns' (exemplified by Joyce), with some additional remarks on the influence of modern

EDWARDIANS AND GEORGIANS

In a series of essays in the early 1920s Woolf distinguished between the focus and methods of the 'Edwardian' novelists H. G. Wells, Arnold Bennett, John Galsworthy and Hugh Walpole, and those of the younger generation of 'Georgians' or 'Moderns', represented by Joyce, T. S. Eliot, E. M. Forster and Lytton Strachey. Describing the former as 'materialists' she argues that they fail to capture reality because they think it consists only of social and material phenomena, and do not pay attention to the internal experience of the consciousness, unlike the 'Moderns' who are more interested in the 'spiritual' quality of life (by which Woolf means the mind or consciousness). For such a subtle critic as Woolf, this is an astonishing oversimplification, but offers a classic example of what was a common tactic on the part of the 'moderns': defining their own 'newness' against the straw-dog of an out-dated and supposedly naïve realism. The 'Edwardians' were in fact more receptive to the experiments of the younger generation, despite their departure from their own literary values, than the influence of Woolf's account might suggest. Wells' review of Joyce's *A Portrait of the Artist as a Young Man*, for example, which appeared in the *Nation* in February 1917, was insightful if not entirely positive, drawing attention to the cinematic quality of the writing (Deming, 1970: 87). Bennett persevered with reluctance through *Ulysses*, declaring that its originality never quite made up for 'its pervading difficult dullness', but nevertheless gave high praise to Molly Bloom's monologue, which he described as an unsurpassable representation of feminine psychology (221).

Russian fiction (Woolf had written several reviews of translations of Dostoevsky, and the Hogarth Press itself published a number of other Russian translations, including Chekhov's *Notebooks* in 1921). Woolf's rejection of the Edwardian novel clearly echoes Henry James' earlier critique. Wells, Bennett and Galsworthy, she argues, spend their creative energy 'proving the solidity, the *likeness* to life, of the story' (my emphasis), yet amidst this abundance of external detail fail to capture life itself. Rather than concentrating on external events and scene, she asserts, modern novels should be concerned instead with the life of the mind, in all its conscious, subconscious and unconscious workings. The writer needs to break from the limits of materialist realism, and find new methods and forms for representing this life in all its immediacy and multiplicity.

Then follows one of the most frequently quoted passages of Woolf's critical and fictional writing:

> Look within and life, it seems, is very far from being 'like this'. Examine for a moment an ordinary mind on an ordinary day. The mind receives a myriad impressions – trivial, fantastic, evanescent, or engraved with the sharpness of steel. From all sides they come, an incessant shower of innumerable atoms; and as they fall, as they shape themselves into the life of Monday or Tuesday, the accent falls differently from of old . . . Life is not a series of gig-lamps symmetrically arranged; life is a luminous halo, a semi-transparent envelope surrounding us from the beginning of consciousness to the end. Is it not the task of the novelist, to convey this varying, this unknown and uncircumscribed spirit, whatever aberration or complexity it may display, with as little mixture of the alien and external as possible. (*E* IV: 160)

The lines that immediately follow, however, show that she has in fact been summarising what she supposes to be the strategy of writers such as Joyce (whom she names) and Richardson (whom she doesn't name) rather than her own narrative style, and indeed spends much of the rest of the essay (from this point on little changed from 'Modern Novels') in distancing herself from the literary method that she sees it giving rise to:

> It is, at any rate, in some such fashion as this that we seek to define the quality which distinguishes the work of several young writers, among whom Mr. James

Joyce is the most notable, from that of their predecessors. They attempt to come closer to life, and to preserve more sincerely and exactly what interests and moves them, even if to do so they must discard most of the conventions which are commonly observed by the novelist. Let us record the atoms as they fall upon the mind in the order in which they fall, let us trace the pattern, however disconnected and incoherent in appearance, which each sight or incident scores upon the consciousness. Any one who has read *The Portrait of the Artist as a Young Man* or, what promises to be a far more interesting work, *Ulysses* . . . , will have hazarded some theory of this nature as to Mr. Joyce's intention. (161)

Modern novels such as *Ulysses*, which Woolf explicitly refers to in the essay, and *The Tunnel*, which she doesn't, but had read and reviewed earlier in 1919, were attempting, she argues, to capture this aspect of life. She then cites the 'Hades' section of *Ulysses*, in which Leopold Bloom attends the funeral of Paddy Dignam, as epitomising this emphasis on 'the quick of the mind' in all its immediacy. Take, for example, the following passage:

Martin Cunningham emerged from a sidepath, talking gravely.

Solicitor, I think. I know his face. Menton. John Henry, solicitor, commissioner for oaths and affidavits. Dignam used to be in his office. Matt Dillon's long ago. Jolly Mat convivial evenings. Cold fowl, cigars, the Tantalus glasses. Heart of gold really. Yes, Menton. Got his rag out that evening on the bowling green because I sailed inside him. Pure fluke of mine: the bias. Why he took such a rooted dislike to me. Hate at first sight. Molly and Floey Dillon linked under the lilactree, laughing. Fellow always like that, mortified if women are by.

Got a dinge in the side of his hat. Carriage probably.

— Excuse me, sir, Mr Bloom said beside them.

They stopped.

— Your hat is a little crushed, Mr Bloom said, pointing.

John Henry Menton stared at him for an instant without moving. (*U*:146)

Bloom's process of identifying Cunningham's companion, and his half-formed and fragmentary reflections on their past acquaintance, occur in an instant yet reveal to the reader far more than the simple remark about the hat that he finally makes. 'If we want life itself,' Woolf writes in

'Modern Fiction', 'here surely we have it' (*E* IV: 161). The only problem, we discover as we read further, is that actually Woolf is far from sure that we do 'have it'; because something else, found only in what she calls 'the dark places of psychology', is still missing (162).

Woolf ascribes to Joyce a subjective impressionism that aims to record directly the movements of the mind, seemingly unmediated by any artistic selection or form. It is a method, however, with which she is not entirely in agreement, because it is *so* concentrated on one individual mind that it refuses to acknowledge the interaction of consciousness with the world around it. 'Is it the method that inhibits the creative power?' she asks, 'Is it due to the method that we feel . . . centred in a self which, in spite of its tremor of susceptibility, never embraces or creates what is outside itself and beyond?' (162). In April 1919, when she initially wrote this summation of Joyce's method, Woolf would have read only the first sections of *Ulysses*, but that it survives in the 1925 essay (indeed with the qualification that the success of the method is less important than the psychological reality expressed *removed*) suggests that her opinion did not improve as she read further. While commending Joyce's courage in discarding all novelistic conventions in his attempt to depict life itself freely and sincerely, she decides that for the same reason he too ultimately fails. Woolf's at best grudging response to the work of Joyce and Richardson is often put down to a mixture of professional rivalry and genteel snobbery. Yet her criticism does also represent both a formal and ideological rejection of their focus. For Woolf their detailed recording of conscious impressions missed the 'profundity' of the soul demonstrated by Russian fiction. It is the method of both the Edwardians *and* the Moderns that she critiques in 'Modern Fiction'; the accumulative materialism of the one, in whose novels 'life escapes', and the unrelenting egoism of the other, in whose work it is 'confined and shut in'.

When 'Modern Novels' appeared in the *TLS* in April 1919, Woolf had not yet written any of her own major works. Indeed *Night and Day*, published later in the year, seemed to some reviewers to be *more* conventional than the earlier *The Voyage Out* (1915). In a series of short fictional sketches, however, she was testing out the concerns increasingly evident in her literary criticism. 'The Mark on the Wall' (1917), 'Kew Gardens' (1917) and 'An Unwritten Novel' (1919) were all composed as diversions from work on *Night and Day*. 'I daresay one ought to invent a completely new form', she wrote of her efforts to force her writing into the accepted shape of the novel, '[a]nyhow it is very amusing to try with these short things, and the greatest mercy to be able to do what one likes'. What Woolf meant by doing what she liked was a refusal to portray time, plot or character in the expected way of the novel. Instead she takes trivial incidents from everyday life and explores their hidden significance. Her method is similar to her description of that of Chekhov's short stories at the end of 'Modern Novels':

> The emphasis is laid upon such unexpected places that at first it seems as if there were no emphasis at all; and then, as the eyes accustom themselves to twilight and discern the shapes of things in a room we see how complete the story is, how profound, and how truly in obedience to his vision Tchekov has chosen this, that, and the other, and placed them together to compose something new. (*E* III: 35)

In the first story the narrator muses on the possible cause of 'a small round mark, black upon a white wall' (*MW*: 3), and then moves onto a rush of further associations, until the reverie is broken by a voice abruptly announcing on its way out to buy a newspaper that the mark is in fact a snail. The entire episode encompasses no more than a minute, despite the multiple movements in thought it has contained. Amidst the rush of modern life, however, this experience stands out in its reflective intensity, seeming to transcend the standard linearity of passing time and convey infinity in the 'luminous halo' of a moment. 'Kew Gardens', by contrast, presents an impressionistic, external scene rather than a reflective, internal one, shifting between the insects and humans that hover beneath the July sun. The narrative moves freely between individual perspectives, and in and out of an external and internal point of view, in a manner that reminded readers of the effects of the film camera Winifred Holtby noted, for example, that 'To let the perspective shift from high to low, from huge to microscopic, to let figures of people, insects, aeroplanes, flowers pass across the vision and melt away – these are devices common enough to another form of art. These are the tricks of the cinema' (Holtby, 1978: 111). In 'An Unwritten Novel', Woolf changes tactic once again, to concentrate on the mystery of identity, the narrator prompted by a brief remark to reconstruct imaginatively the life of a woman travelling in the same railway carriage, only to find when they reach their destination that her assumptions have been entirely misjudged. Taken together, all three of these short pieces formed the foundation of Woolf's subsequent aesthetic. In a diary entry for January 1920, she records 'having this afternoon arrived at some idea of a new form for a new novel', continuing '[w]hether I'm sufficiently mistress of things – that's the doubt; but conceive mark on the wall, K G. & unwritten novel taking hands & dancing in unity' (*D* II: 14). The intensity of moments in which the mystery of character is briefly overcome and a connection between self and world is achieved, becomes one of the key features of her redefinition of reality in the novel, as we will see in the following chapter. 'I have found out how to begin (at 40) to say something in my own voice', she wrote on the publication of *Jacob's Room* in July 1922, '& that interests me so much that I feel I can go ahead without praise' (186).

SUMMARY

The focus of this chapter has been on the formalist impulse of the modernist novel; the endeavour to reflect the modern world in not only the subject but also the method and style of literary representation. The question of the nature of reality, and how to capture it in fiction, lies at the foundation of the modernist novel, for which the debate over narrative technique in the early twentieth century provides a key context. Keenly aware that 'life' was more various than normative generic conventions tended to make it seem, some writers began to feel that the novel's ability to render and explore experience had been pushed as far as possible within its current model. Modern times and modern ideas demanded new forms and new literary techniques. Neither Joyce, Richardson nor Woolf was anti-realist (indeed contemporary reviewers typically drew attention to the *heightened* realism of their work). However, they didn't believe that a concentration on the external aspects of life conveyed the fullness of human experience, or that the presentation of a character's thoughts and emotions by an all-seeing omniscient narrator (both typical of the formal strategies of the nineteenth-century novel) could offer a representation of modern life that was at all 'realistic'. Indeed by implying that it was able accurately to represent contemporary reality, and failing to acknowledge its own artifice, the traditional form of the novel would end up misrepresenting it. The modernist novel thus diverges from the classical realist novel in two main ways. First, although it still aims at the direct representation of human experience, it differs in its understanding of what constitutes that experience. Second, it is sceptical about the possibility of communicating this experience objectively, and therefore denies any obligation to provide the reader with descriptive or 'external' detail about character, time and place. While Joyce, Woolf and Richardson's specific experimentations with the narrative form and focus of the novel genre were independent and distinct, together they were recognised by their contemporaries (whether celebratory or hostile) as pioneers of a new subjective realism: exchanging the traditional representation of a character's social development for the expression of his or her individual psychological being, the external description of scene for the internal revelation of consciousness, and chronological narrative and dramatic plot for the flux of momentary thoughts and impressions that constitute mental life.

2

CHARACTER AND
CONSCIOUSNESS

In the previous chapter we examined Joyce, Richardson and Woolf's belief that modern fiction needed to break from previous generic conventions in order to express modern life properly, and their initial exploration of the possibilities of a subjective as opposed to a social and mimetic realism. A fundamental aspect of their new realism was a shift of focus in the representation of character and consciousness, in the light of the pervasive influence of psychological thought at the turn of the century, and how it repositioned the individual in relation to the world around him. This is not to say that earlier writers were not responsive to or concerned with the pulse and vagaries of the human psyche. Yet however much the indeterminacy of psychological reality might have been recognised within the eighteenth- or nineteenth-century novel, the understanding of identity and selfhood nevertheless remained framed within a fundamental belief in an empirically verifiable, universally understood, socially and economically defined world.

Since the 1880s philosophers and psychologists had been popularising an introspective approach to the analysis of mental life, or as the psychologist William James described it in his groundbreaking and hugely popular *Principles of Psychology* in 1890: 'the looking into our own minds and reporting what we there discover' (James, 1981: 185). His brother Henry James would take up a similar principle in the novel, placing the focus of the narrative within the perspective of a single character, just as the development of an 'impressionist' aesthetic in the works of Joseph Conrad and Ford Madox Ford would highlight the disjunction between public and private experience. By the time that Joyce, Richardson and Woolf were struggling with how to portray modern consciousness in the early 1910s, the notion of the self as primarily stable and rational had been exchanged for something far more variable and intangible, subject not only to its particular biases and perspective but also to the more mysterious workings of the mind and the unconscious.

THE STREAM OF CONSCIOUSNESS

A focus on the subjective consciousness of the individual mind has become one of the defining features of the modernist novel, identified as both its principal theme and dominant technique. The term is derived from William James' description of the way in which thoughts, perceptions, memories, associations and sensations in all their multitude are experienced by the mind.

STREAM OF CONSCIOUSNESS

In *Principles of Psychology* (1890), William James described conscious experience as continuous and unbroken: 'It is nothing jointed; it flows. A "river" or "stream" are the metaphors by which it is most naturally described. In talking of it hereafter, let us call it the stream of thought, of consciousness, or of subjective life'. Unlike the intuitive, anti-representational quality of duration, the stream of consciousness as James conceives it here refers to the never-ending associative flow of our conscious or half-conscious thoughts and perceptions and feelings, the activity of the mind that we are always at least vaguely sensible of. The concept of stream of consciousness is often collapsed in literary criticism with the narrative technique of interior monologue, but it would be more accurate to think of it as the active subjective life that interior monologue, in an attempt to represent it, imitates in the symbolic form of language. For the difficulty of defining stream of consciousness as a single narrative style however see Humphrey, 1954; Friedman, 1955. For the recent resurgence of the term within the philosophy of mind see Strawson, 1994; Dainton, 2000.

To understand some of the different kinds of narrative focus subsumed by the stream-of-consciousness label, it is useful to have some awareness of the ideas that dominated psychological and philosophical thought at the beginning of the twentieth century. A contemporary reader might be likely to assume that the psychological focus of the modernist novel resulted from the impact of the psychoanalysis of Sigmund Freud (1856–1939). In the first decades of the twentieth century, however, the celebrity mind of the moment was the French philosopher Henri Bergson (1859–1941), whose theories of consciousness, the creative impulse and the nature of time acquired an unprecedented popular following and profoundly influenced the European intellectual and artistic scene.

In Bergson's view it was impossible to demonstrate what the self was like beneath the composed surface of social identity, because in transforming the internal workings of the individual mind into the external structures of language the qualitative aspect of consciousness was lost. '[T]he rough and ready word', he declared in his essay 'Time and Free Will', automatically 'overwhelms or at least covers over the delicate and fugitive impressions of our individual consciousness' (Bergson, 2001: 132). However, he suggested,

HENRI BERGSON

Bergson revolutionised philosophical thought with his emphasis on intuition over reason as the means by which 'reality' is to be understood. At the foundation of his ideas is the argument that there are two forms of conscious life; in the first psychic states are experienced intensely and qualitatively as an organic, fluid whole, whereas in the second they are broken up and made quantitatively identifiable. This is because intuitive or fundamental experience can only be perceived at the level of rational or intellectual consciousness by being transformed into objectifying, spatial or symbolic form. At best, however, this can provide only an artificial imitation of internal life. Aware of the implications of his argument for philosophical analysis itself, Bergson's methodological approach and terminology is typically imagistic and metaphorical. Bergson was awarded the Nobel Prize for Literature in 1927. His key works are *Time and Free Will* (1889; tr. 1910), *Matter and Memory* (1896; tr. 1910) and *Creative Evolution* (1907; tr. 1911).

> if some bold novelist, tearing aside the cleverly woven curtain of our conventional ego, shows us under this appearance of logic a fundamental absurdity, under this juxtaposition of simple states an infinite permeation of a thousand impressions which have ceased to exist the instant they are named, we commend him for having known us better than we know ourselves. (133)

It is this challenge that Richardson took up in writing the infinite consciousness of Miriam Henderson. May Sinclair, for example, applying the concept of stream of consciousness to literature for the first time in her review of *Pilgrimage* in 1918, observed: 'It is just life going on and on. It is Miriam Henderson's stream of consciousness going on and on. And in neither is there any discernible beginning or middle or end' (Kime Scott, 1990: 444). This unrelenting focus on the movements of a single mind, Sinclair argues, resulted in Richardson's new kind of psychological realism: 'In identifying herself with this life, which is Miriam's stream of consciousness, Miss Richardson produces her effect of being the first, of getting closer to reality than any of our novelists who are trying so desperately to get close' (444). Although Sinclair was describing Richardson's *subject-matter*, however – Miriam's thoughts and perceptions – the phrase was soon taken up by literary criticism in vague reference to the internal narrative *style* of the modernist novel. As such it has become unhelpfully homogenising, Richardson, for example, repeatedly declaring her frustration at being pigeon-holed with Joyce and Woolf as 'stream of consciousness' writers, while their specific methods for representing quite different types of consciousness went overlooked.

For an instance of Richardson's method, consider the following passage from the opening of *The Tunnel* (1919), the longest and in terms of the representation of Miriam's stream of consciousness arguably the most experimental of the *Pilgrimage* novels:

> She was surprised now at her familiarity with the detail of the room . . . that idea of visiting places in dreams. It was something more than that . . . all the real part of your life has a real dream in it; some of the real dream part of you coming true. You know in advance when you are really following your life. These things are familiar because reality is here. Coming events cast *light*. It is like dropping everything and walking backwards to something you know is there. However far

you go out you come back . . . I am back now where I was before I began trying to do things like other people. I left home to get here. None of those things can touch me here. . . . The sight of her luggage piled on the other side of the fire-place drew her forward into the dimness. There was a small chest of drawers, battered and almost paintless, but with two long drawers and two small ones and a white cover on which stood a little looking-glass framed in polished pine . . . and a small, yellow wardrobe with a deep drawer under the hanging part, and a little drawer in the rickety little washstand and another above the dusty cupboard of the little mahogany sideboard. I'll paint the bright part of the ceiling; scrolls of leaves. . . . (P II: 13–14)

Miriam arrives here in the boarding-house room that will be her London home for the following ten years. Several layers of conscious awareness are interwoven: the immediate intense feeling of familiarity, only *intuitively* sensed and therefore articulated in fragmentary sentences, which moves into the conscious, *perceptual* impression of the look of the room, conveyed in highly visual description, and finally the *intentional* thought about painting the ceiling, in which the narrative shifts to the conscious first-person but without the direction of speech marks or the third-person insertion of 'she thought'. The ellipses convey the associative flow of her mind, but also the wordlessness of moments that remain untranslated into either the language of thought or external imagery.

If Sinclair celebrated such direct psychological realism, however, other reviewers, generally far from unsympathetic to avant-garde writing, found such extended passages of dense and seemingly trivial interior monologue exasperatingly meaningless. For Katherine Mansfield, reviewing *The Tunnel* in 1919, Miriam registers every detail of her immediate sensory experience with a mental recording power that is impressive but ultimately little more than just a technical feat:

'What cannot I do with this mind of mine!' one can fancy her saying. 'What can I not see and remember and express!' There are times when she seems deliberately to set it a task, just for the joy of realizing again how brilliant a machine it is, and we, too, share her admiration for its power of absorbing. Anything that goes into her mind she can summon forth again, and there it is, complete in every detail, with nothing taken away from it – and nothing added. (Kime Scott, 1990: 309)

Mansfield's description of the mechanical aspect of Miriam's consciousness compares interestingly to Bergson's own warning in the conclusion to 'Time and Free Will' that attempts to represent the qualitative multiplicity of psychic states in language will only be able to imitate 'the process by which nervous matter procures reflex actions', and thus result in 'automatism' (Bergson, 2001: 237). Richardson's technique, Mansfield argues, concentrates only on Miriam's surface perceptions, as they occur and as she is consciously aware of them, but fails to make this suggestive of a more continuous sense of self. Woolf and Mansfield were professional friends and rivals before the latter's premature death in 1923, and Woolf's own anonymous review of *The Tunnel* for the *TLS* in February 1919 voiced similar reservations about its ultimately superficial quality. 'That Miss Richardson gets so far as to achieve a sense of reality far greater than that produced by the ordinary means is undoubted', she notes, 'But, then, which reality is it, the superficial or the profound?' (*E* III: 11). The problem, she thinks, is the nature of Miriam's consciousness, which she again criticises for being more sensory and automatic than reflective: 'Her senses of touch, sight and hearing are all excessively acute. But sensations, impressions, ideas and emotions glance off her, unrelated and unquestioned, without shedding as much hope as we had hoped into the hidden depths' (11).

Mansfield and Woolf's criticism in part derives from the fact that Richardson's focus on the Bergsonian immediacy of Miriam's *consciousness* seemed to work against her development as a *character*. For although Bergson drew attention to a distinction between the conventional ego as understood in relation to the external world and a fundamental self of purely qualitative psychic states, separate from society and language, he yet also acknowledged that without the spatialising impulse of the intellect, our awareness of identity would be impossible, relying as it does on a sense of continuity that necessarily demands the distinction of past, present and future. 'She has no memory', Mansfield states of Miriam, 'It is true that Life is sometimes very swift and breathless, but not always. If we are to be truly alive there are large pauses in which we creep away into our caves of contemplation' (Kime Scott, 1990: 309). Yet Miriam clings to the surface preoccupations of her life from day to day exactly in order to *avoid* thinking about the more fundamental issues of her past, present and future. The enforced departure from her comfortable middle-class upbringing in *Pointed Roofs*, the hints of Mrs Henderson's illness in *Backwater* and the oblique allusion to her suicide at the end of *Honeycomb* are fundamental to the representation of Miriam in *The Tunnel*, although they would seem to have been entirely missed by contemporary reviewers. For Richardson's project was the faithful portrayal of reality as experienced by an intelligent but traumatised and self-protective young woman, watching her eagerness for life slip away amidst the drudgery of work and physical exhaustion, trying to squeeze every sensation from moments of respite in the quiet of her room, the impersonal embrace of the London streets or the rapid passing of evenings and weekends with friends. Writing *through* Miriam's harried consciousness would require not the kind of lengthy reflections on the past indulged in and enjoyed by Proust's leisured, wealthy Marcel, but instead her desperate attempt to suppress and forget it. Yet that is not to say that that past was not significant, or indeed implicated within her emotions and acts in the present, however obliquely.

A MODERN HERO

Although Joyce and Richardson were regularly cited alongside each other as purveyors of the new 'stream-of-consciousness' novel, no single character or consciousness dominates *Ulysses* in the way that Miriam Henderson does throughout *Pilgrimage*. For while the first half of the novel uses the recognisable technique of interior monologue to present the thoughts and impressions of Stephen Dedalus and Leopold Bloom, the diverse styles and idioms with which he became preoccupied in the later sections by contrast reduce Stephen and Bloom as individual characters to the wider mechanics of the novel as a whole. If any single consciousness dominates *Ulysses* it becomes that of Joyce himself, who far from effacing his authorial control behind the thoughts and perceptions of his characters, demonstrated it with every change of style, repetition of phrase or image, or symbolic parallel or juxtaposition.

When Joyce began writing *Ulysses* in 1914 he was already conceiving the novel as a modern epic, a parodic 'Odyssey on the Liffey', but his concern seems to have been firmly with the *character* of his modern hero.

Joyce told Georges Borach, one of his language students in Zurich, that he thought the story of Odysseus was 'the most human in world literature', and Frank Budgen that he was the most 'complete all-round character' (Potts, 1979: 70; Ellmann, 1982: 435). 'Ulysses', he elaborated, 'is son to Laertes, but he is father to Telemachus, husband to Penelope, lover of Calypso, companion in arms of the Greek warriors around Troy, and King of Ithaca' (435). As a result he seemed to Joyce more humane and three-dimensional than the other heroes of Greek myth. His own Ulysses, he told Budgen, would be similarly 'complete'. Leopold Bloom, an advertising salesman whose wife is cheating on him, who buys a kidney for his breakfast, picks his toe-nails and masturbates in public, may seem an unlikely parallel for the wily Greek. Bloom's life, presented in full prosaic detail, seems outstandingly ordinary. But at the same time it is this ordinariness that the reader is asked to be interested in, and to recognise as the extraordinary reality of life. For Joyce is not suggesting that Bloom be *equated* with his mythic prototype, and thus elevated or ridiculed by the comparison. Instead we are to recognise in his character and circumstances the all-round man that Ulysses also is, revealing during the events of his day in Dublin his essential honesty and kindness, his prudence and wit, his physical and emotional needs and desires, and also his sense of exile and isolation, in the same way that Ulysses did in the adventures that took him on his long journey home to Ithaca. 'Joyce's first question when I had read a completed episode or when he had read out a passage of an uncompleted one', Budgen later recalled, 'was always: "How does Bloom strike you?" . . . Technical considerations, problems of Homeric correspondence, the chemistry of the human body, were secondary matters' (Budgen, 1972: 106–7).

Budgen's stress on Bloom as an individual here is interesting, contrasting sharply with the warning by Stuart Gilbert, another of Joyce's 'spokesmen', against the assumption that 'the striking psychological realism of the narrative' meant that Joyce's interest was in the delineation of character. Although in most novels, Gilbert asserts, 'the reader's interest is aroused and his attention held by the presentation of dramatic situations, of problems deriving from conduct or character and the reactions of the fictitious personages among themselves', this is fundamentally not the case in *Ulysses* (Gilbert, 1930: 20). His emphasis on Joyce's *refusal* to accord Stephen, Bloom or Molly such individual agency is worth quoting at length:

> The personages of *Ulysses* are not fictitious and its true significance does not lie in problems of conduct or character. After reading *Ulysses* we do not ask ourselves: 'Should Stephen Dedalus have done this? Ought Mr Bloom to have said that? Should Mrs Bloom have refrained?' All these people are as they must be; they act, we see, according to some *lex eterna*, an ineluctable condition of their very existence. . . . The meaning of *Ulysses*, for it has a meaning and is not merely a photographic 'slice of life' – far from it – is not to be sought in any analysis of the acts of the protagonists or the mental make-up of the characters; it is, rather, implicit in the technique of the various episodes, in nuances of language, in the thousand and one correspondences and allusions with which the book is studded. . . . The attitude of the author of *Ulysses* to his personages and their activities is one of serene detachment; all is grist to his mill, which, like God's, grinds slowly and exceedingly small. (20–1)

Gilbert's study was written, with Joyce's authority, with the intention of emphasising the importance of the structural framework of Homeric and other correspondences that Budgen downplayed and indeed a majority of readers entirely missed. Their opposing accounts reflect their own critical preferences as much as any guidance from Joyce himself (Budgen's realist and concerned with character and environment, Gilbert's structural and concerned with style and technique), but they are also to an extent justified by the ambiguities of the text itself. For while Joyce may have conceived *Ulysses* as an epic tale of a *modern* 'complete, all-round character' ('He's a cultured allroundman, Bloom is', Lenehan states in the 'Wandering Rocks' episode), in the multiplying stylistic strategies that he developed over the six years in which he was writing the novel, the representation and focus on that character altered significantly.

The first nine episodes of *Ulysses*, from 'Telemachus' to 'Scylla and Charybdis', constitute what Joyce described as his 'initial style' (*LJJ* I: 129), in which a concern with character seems uppermost. Direct internal monologue is interspersed with external conversation and a hardly noticeable third-person narrator situating the characters and events, to create the illusion that the reader is following Stephen or

Bloom's 'stream of consciousness'. 'I try to give the unspoken, unacted thoughts of people in the way they occur', Joyce told Budgen (Budgen, 1972: 92). Rather than claim to have originated this technique, as subsequent commentators are inclined to suggest, Joyce always credited his discovery of interior monologue to a little-known novel, *Les lauriers sont coupés* (1887), by the French writer Édouard Dujardin. Having initially read the book in 1903 he remembered being intrigued by the author's technique, and during the drafting of the early episodes of *Ulysses* in 1917 wrote to Dujardin to ask for a new copy to study. Joyce evolves Dujardin's original method, however, in his adaptation of the tone and imagery of a character's internal monologue according to the influence of internal and external stimuli. 'In my book the body lives in and moves through space and is the home of a full human personality,' Joyce told Budgen in 1918, '[t]he words I write are adapted to express first one of its functions then another' (21). In 'Lestrygonians', he notes as an example, which follows Bloom through the hunger and then surfeit of his lunch hour:

> the stomach dominates and the rhythm of the episode is that of the peristaltic movement . . . Walking towards his lunch my hero, Leopold Bloom, thinks of his wife, and says to himself, 'Molly's legs are out of plumb.' At another time of day he might have expressed the same thought without any under-thought of food. But I want the reader to understand always through suggestion rather than direct statement. (21)

This strategy continued relatively straightforwardly through all of the first nine episodes of the novel. Having finished 'Scylla and Charybdis', however, Joyce marked the manuscript: 'End of First Part of "Ulysses", New Years' Eve 1918' (Groden, 1977: 17). It is worth noting that Joyce had only written a third of *Ulysses* by the time it began serialisation in the *Little Review* in 1918, from then on producing each new episode only shortly before the next monthly publication, and revising them continually up to 1922, adding numerous small details, expanding the symbolic parallels and in some cases dramatically altering narrative style. These changes, along with the removal of the Homeric chapter headings that had been included with the serial instalments, meant that the final 1922 text provided a very different reading experience from that of the serialised episodes. Abandoning interior monologue as the dominant narrative style, Joyce began to reassert an overt authorial omniscience, taking up and parodying a range of narrative and other representational styles. In revising the first half of the novel for the final published text, moreover, he returned to the Bloom episodes to include more 'realistic' details but also to elaborate the developing system of schematic parallels. The result is a tour de force of stylistic virtuosity in which language is pushed to the limits of its ability to express experience, and shown up for the clichés and rhetoric to which it largely descends, but in which the reader's intimacy with the minds of Stephen and Bloom, even in the first half of the novel, is arguably reduced.

The reason for Joyce's abandonment of the use of direct internal monologue, and the consequent downplaying of the individuality of identity in *Ulysses*, is perhaps hinted at by his comment to Budgen following Ezra Pound's suggestion that Stephen be returned to the foreground as the focus of the narrative. Joyce had become bored with his recreation of his former self: 'Stephen no longer interests me', he observed, '[h]e has a shape that can't be changed' (Budgen, 1972: 107). He also felt that he had taken the focus on a single inward-looking consciousness in the manner of *A Portrait of the Artist as a Young Man* as far as he could. The modern interest of *Ulysses*, Joyce declared, was in 'the subterranean forces, those hidden tides which govern everything and run humanity counter to the apparent flood' (Hart, 1974: 54). His statement implies a move away from the stream of consciousness of the individual mind, to the conception of deeper, underlying currents of collective human existence, and is an indication of the evolution in Joyce's conception of character across the writing of *A Portrait* and *Ulysses*. The former, like Richardson's *Pilgrimage*, is a *bildungsroman*, its very purpose to follow an individual's journey to self-identity. The function of characters in *Ulysses* is to represent a fundamental unity to human existence across time and space. They are thus significant not so much as individuals, although they *are* individuals, but as the modern representatives of human qualities and experiences constantly recycled and repeated from the beginning of history until its end. Joyce would extend this strategy even further in *Finnegans Wake*, his book about the human consciousness by night rather than by day, of which he commented, '[t]here are in a way no characters. It's like a dream' (Ellmann, 1982: 696). In the dream narrative of the subconscious or unconscious mind, the self-consciousness of the ego (and thus of individuated character) gives way to what Joyce suggests are the universal and eternal 'memories' of human instinct.

The denial of not only the guiding voice of a reliable omniscient narrator, but also the focalising point of view of a central narrative consciousness in the second half of the novel, is in part what makes *Ulysses* such a challenge for readers. Used to the liberal humanist tradition of the English novel, with its interest in the uniqueness of identity and an innate self (however experimentally portrayed), our immediate impulse is to see the characters in *Ulysses* as rounded, fully realised individuals, to whose essence of thought we have privileged access through the technique of interior monologue. Joyce, however, was breaking not only with the novelistic conventions of plot and linear chronology but also the individualisation of the self in a way that Richardson, for example, did not. Miriam Henderson seems to possess a strongly bounded individual consciousness for which language is a tool of self-expression. Joyce reveals language to be what actually constitutes that consciousness.

However, it does perhaps explain why that consciousness seemed unsatisfactory as a portrayal of character, despite its seeming all-inclusiveness. Holbrook Jackson, for example, said of Bloom that

> [y]ou live with him minute by minute; go with him everywhere, physically and mentally; you are made privy to his thoughts and emotions . . . until you know his whole life through and through; know him, in fact, better than you know any other being in art and literature.

But, he concluded in some bewilderment, '[i]t is not clear why he troubled to introduce him' (Deming, 1970: 199). Meanwhile even T. S. Eliot, while celebrating what he defined as Joyce's 'mythic method' in print, observed to Virginia Woolf in private that his technique ultimately failed as a mode of characterisation, stating that 'Bloom told one nothing', and that 'this new method of giving the psychology proves to my mind that it doesn't work. It doesn't tell as much as some casual glance from outside often tells' (*D* II: 203).

That the delineation of individual character in *Ulysses* was increasingly subordinated in Joyce's writing to a philosophical belief in generic humanity and an aesthetic display of technical virtuosity seems to have been generally agreed upon by both Joyce's supporters and his detractors. One of the most fundamental critiques was by his former drinking partner Wyndham Lewis. 'Joyce is above all things, essentially the craftsman', Lewis declared in *Time and Western Man* (1927), his polemical attack on what he regarded as the subjectivist trend dominating 1920s Western culture, '[w]hat stimulates him is *ways of doing things*, and technical processes, and not *things to be done*' (Lewis, 1993: 88). The detail and form of representation preoccupied Joyce more, in other words, than what was being represented. 'Where a multitude of little details or some obvious idiosyncracy are concerned, he may be said to be observant', Lewis notes, 'but the secret of an entire organism escapes him' (99). The result, he argues, is that Joyce concentrates on either caricatured fragments of personality or general human tendencies, creating 'with a mass of detail a superficial appearance of life' in which people are yet 'mechanical and abstract, the opposite of the living' (99). Lewis accuses Joyce of creating generic types; the Jew (Bloom), the Poet (Stephen), the Irishman (Mulligan), the Englishman (Haines) and the Freudian 'eternal feminine' (Molly). His assertion of the spiritual gulf between these 'walking clichés' (94) and the more simply portrayed yet also more fundamentally human characters of the Russian literary scene continues Woolf's more cautious reservations about the modern method in her essays 'Modern Novels' and 'Modern Fiction'. There she critiqued Joyce (referring to the initial style of *Ulysses*) for focussing his narrative within a consciousness that 'never reaches out or embraces or comprehends what is outside and beyond' (*E* III: 34). In Woolf's eyes, both Joyce and Richardson positioned the reader within the limits of what she described as 'the damned egotistical self' of the author. Her own fiction would be preoccupied not with the self in isolation, but with the mystery of other lives and the fascination of other selves, the 'will-o'-the-wisp' of character, as she described it, who calls softly to the writer, '"My name is Brown. Catch me if you can."' (*E* III: 420).

LOOKING FOR 'MRS BROWN'

'No generation since the world began has known quite so much about character as our generation', Woolf observed in a lecture given to the

Cambridge Heretics Society in May 1924 (*E* III: 504). Published under the title of 'Character in Fiction' in T. S. Eliot's magazine *Criterion* in July, and as 'Mr Bennett and Mrs Brown' by the Hogarth Press in October, it offered her response to the criticism by Arnold Bennett that she was more interested in innovative technique than the creation of believable characters. 'I have seldom read a cleverer book than Virginia Woolf's *Jacob's Room*', Bennett had written in his article 'Is the Novel Decaying?' in March 1923, '[b]ut the characters do not vitally survive in the mind because the author has been obsessed by details of originality and clever-ness'. That Bennett could argue that the modern generation failed to create convincing characters, while Woolf asserted that it understood more about character than ever before, indicates the disparity between their conceptions of identity and models of characterisation. For Bennett a solidly delineated social and material context was integral to believable character. For Woolf this typically conflicted with, or simply left out, the subjective essence of the self. Her defence unsurprisingly continued the attack on Edwardian fiction she had begun in 'Modern Novels' in 1919, set within the broader argument that the twentieth century had witnessed a change in the conception of character that necessitated a change in methods of literary characterisation.

'[O]n or about December 1910 human character changed', Woolf declares polemically towards the beginning of 'Character in Fiction' (*E* III: 421). It is a statement that has provoked much critical discussion about why Woolf might have chosen such a specific date (the death of Edward VII, the opening of the first exhibition of post-impressionist art, the political and social unrest marked by the rise of the suffragette move-ment and the Welsh miners' strike), although her point from the post-war perspective of 1924 is probably that this accumulation of events can be seen as marking the end of an era of stability and ushering in one of con-flict and crisis. The present suddenly seemed cut off from the past, alien-ated by the war and with it the loss of values and beliefs that had underpinned previous assumptions about a permanent and universal structure to life. A glance at her essay 'How it Strikes a Contemporary', published in the *TLS* the previous year, makes it clear that Woolf's argu-ment is not so much that human character itself has changed, however, but rather the context within which it is shaped and understood. Writers such as Jane Austen or Walter Scott, she argues there, used tools appropriate to their perspective on the world, and although they might have ignored the '[s]hades and subtleties' of individual perception (*E* III: 358) that preoccupied the contemporary novel, this was because they possessed a conviction about man's place in the universe that allowed them to produce complete fictional worlds. 'To believe that your impressions hold good for others', Woolf asserts, 'is to be released from the cramp and confinement of personality' (*E* III: 358). The modern writer no longer believes in such generalisation, however, and thinks the only material he can faithfully represent is the fragmentary impressions of his own subjective experience. If the essence of life was no longer to be understood in terms of an external reality, then the traditional means of repre-

MR BENNETT AND MRS BROWN

In 'Character in Fiction' Woolf responds to Bennett's critique of *Jacob's Room* with a satirical anecdote in which he, Wells and Galsworthy are depicted as travellers in a railway carriage attempting to sum up the character of the unassuming elderly lady in the corner, Mrs Brown. The Edwardian novelist, Woolf complains, would not be interested in Mrs Brown herself as she appears in the corner of the railway carriage. They would concentrate instead on the details of her surroundings, looking 'very powerfully, searchingly, and sympathetically out of the window; at factories, at Utopias, even at the decoration and upholstery of the carriage; but never at her, never at life, never at human nature' (*E* III: 430). Exasperated, she complains that the novels of the Edwardians leave her with a feeling of incompleteness. In that they wrote for a previous age, she admits, they developed conventions of writing that suited their purpose. Where she takes issue is Bennett's use of such conventions as the norm from which to evaluate the methods of novelists in the present, arguing that 'those tools are not our tools, and that business is not our business' (430). Yet having said that she does not entirely advocate the strategies of 'the Moderns' either. The writing of the Georgians, she states, citing Joyce, Eliot and Lytton Strachey as examples (in her lecture she included Richardson but removed all reference to her from the published version), seems to be marked more by the *destruction* of obsolete conventions than the particular success of its experimentation with new forms and methods.

senting characters by relating them to their external surroundings could no longer be of any use. The novelist needed to devise new methods of characterisation, more appropriate to the modern age.

We have already noted Woolf's determination to avoid the egotistic 'stream of consciousness' of Stephen Dedalus and Miriam Henderson in her own fiction. In *Jacob's Room* she put into practice both her critique of the conventions of the past and her reservations about the techniques of her contemporaries. Throughout the first half of *Jacob's Room* external methods of characterisation consistently fail to capture his identity satisfactorily. When Woolf draws again on the motif of the railway carriage to present Jacob as a young man on his way up to Cambridge, the elderly Mrs Norman, given the role of the travelling observer and nervously examining him from behind her newspaper, decides only that he is probably much like her own son. 'Nobody sees anyone as he is', a detached narrative voice declares, 'They see a whole – they see all sorts of things – they see themselves' (*JR*: 36). What they cannot see, and therefore the reader also cannot see, is Jacob as he appears to himself. The narrator next tries to assess Jacob's character from the appearance of his college digs, the significance of this strategy made more apparent when we remember Woolf's attack on the *materialist* focus of the Edwardian novelist in 'Modern Fiction'. There she compares Bennett's novels to perfectly constructed houses in which there is yet no life, the spiritual element of character lost amidst a mass of objective detail. The depiction of Jacob's room similarly serves to confirm rather than resolve the enigma of character:

> Jacob's room had a round table and two low chairs. There were yellow flags in a jar on the mantelpiece; a photograph of his mother; cards from societies with little raised crescents, coats of arms, and initials; notes and pipes; on the table lay paper ruled with a red margin – an essay no doubt – 'Does history consist of the Biographies of Great Men?' There were books enough; very few French books, but then any one who's worth anything reads just what he likes, as the mood takes him, with extravagant enthusiasm. Lives of the Duke of Wellington, for example; Spinoza; the works of Dickens; the Faery Queen; a Greek dictionary with the petals of poppies pressed to silk between the pages; all the Elizabethans. (*JR*: 48–9)

Although there *are* aspects of Jacob's life (and that of any other Cambridge student in the first decade of the twentieth century) that the intruding narrator might infer from this scene, ultimately the quality that makes Jacob himself is missing: 'Listless is the air in an empty room, just swelling the curtain; the flowers in the jar shift. One fibre in the wicker armchair creaks, though no one sits there.' Bennett's complaint is in a way exactly Woolf's point; external narrative techniques fail to construct character adequately. Yet it is as a result of Jacob's ultimate inscrutability that she would also argue he becomes more 'believable' than the comprehensible characters of Edwardian fiction.

Woolf does make the occasional attempt to convey Jacob as he is to himself, as in the following example, in which his direct speech is contrasted with his inner thoughts:

('I'm twenty-two. It's nearly the end of October. Life is thoroughly pleasant, although unfortunately there are a great number of fools about. One must apply oneself to something or other – God knows what. Everything is really very jolly – except getting up in the morning and wearing a tail coat.')

'I say, Bonamy, what about Beethoven?'

('Bonamy is an amazing fellow. He knows practically everything – not more about English literature than I do – but then he's read all those Frenchmen.')

'I rather suspect you're talking rot Bonamy. In spite of what you say, poor old Tennyson. . . . ' (*JR*: 96–7)

While the first-person narrative does indicate the discrepancy between internal consciousness and external appearance, however, the use of parentheses here is awkward and the maintaining of the 'I' form seems false. Perhaps because of this Woolf predominantly takes a different strategy, refusing any internal monologue on Jacob's part and instead building up his external image as a composite of the fragmentary, partial glimpses of other characters. Dramatising the impossibility of ever knowing how another human being conceives and experiences his or her own self, her depiction of a host of secondary characters drawn together by his elusive presence anticipates what would become her distinctive style of internal narration. The cry of 'Jacob! Jacob!' that reverberates throughout the book is yet here as much that of writer and reader as it is of the other characters, all pursuing in vain the *real* Jacob. Who is the *real* Jacob, the *real* Mrs Brown? Is it possible to move beyond the unknowable otherness of another human being? In what ways might individual consciousness be rendered in the portrayal of fictional character? Is it even possible to depict life as it is for another human being? These are some of the questions Woolf persistently poses in her fictional and non-fictional writing in the early 1920s.

THE STORY OF A LIFE

How to capture 'Mrs Brown', 'the spirit we live by, life itself' (*E* III: 436), was a question that dominated Woolf's thought from her earliest biographical reviews for the *Cornhill Magazine* and *TLS*. Biography had become a vast and popular field of writing towards the end of the nineteenth century, in which her father Leslie Stephen, as founding editor of the *Dictionary of National Biography*, took a prominent role. This mammoth historical project epitomised the standard focus of Victorian biography on the great, usually male, names that figured within the key social and political events of national history. Woolf's interest in biography was in part influenced by her father's writings and at the same time a rejection of them. Her concern was with ordinary lives, the Mrs Browns of the world that such accounts left out.

The representation of identity was a purpose in which Woolf regarded the genres of biography and fiction to be closely linked. 'Interest in our selves and in other people's selves', she notes in an essay on 'The Art of Biography', was a relatively recent phenomenon, arising in the eighteenth century alongside the development of biography and the novel, the genres which most serve it (*CE* IV: 224). Where the novel explored imaginary lives, however, biography focussed on the material of fact. She returned to this argument in another essay, 'The New Biography', quoting the assertion by Sidney Lee, her father's successor at the *Dictionary*, that '"[t]he aim of biography . . . is the truthful transmission of personality"' (*E* IV: 473). Herein lies the central problem, she argues, for what the biographer usually means by truth are facts of 'granite-like solidity', the works or events or discoveries that can be recorded, whereas personality is a thing of 'rainbow-like intangibility', less easy to recover (473). In the past, she notes, the result has been an emphasis on the former to the exclusion of the latter, with the effect that although stuffed full of factual truths the majority of biographies in the past failed to include those truths that illuminate personality. With the twentieth century, she declares however, the multi-volume Victorian biography has been exchanged for slimmer studies that include fewer facts and in which the writer's point of view in relation to his subject has altered significantly.

Woolf's description of the 'new biography' at this point starts to look very much like the new novel, combining 'the reality of truth' with 'the freedom, the artistry of fiction' (474). As in the modern novel, in the new biography it is 'man himself' rather than his great deeds that is of primary interest, and the new biographer, frustrated by the restrictions of his conventional focus on fact, therefore borrows from the dramatic techniques of the novel, in order to give a sense of his personality or character. The new biography resembles the new novel for Woolf in another way, however, which is that despite its promise it has not fully succeeded. Having considered the works of both Lytton Strachey (in the first essay) and Harold Nicholson (in the second), she decides that there is not yet a biographer, 'whose art is subtle and bold enough to present the queer amalgamation of dream and reality, that perpetual marriage of granite and rainbow. His method still remains to be discovered' (478). In 'The Art of Biography', however, having critiqued the biographer's ultimate failure to reconcile fact and imagination, Woolf nevertheless suggests that:

> By telling us the true facts, by sifting the little from the big, and shaping the whole so that we perceive the outline, the biographer does more to stimulate the imagination than any poet or novelist save the very greatest. For few poets and novelists are capable of that high degree of tension which gives us reality. But almost any biographer, if he respects facts, can give us much more than another fact to add to our collection. He can give us the creative fact; the fertile fact; the fact that suggests and engenders. (*CE* IV: 227)

The new fiction, she implies, should borrow from biography as much as the new biography does from fiction. For just as the biographer has so far failed to blend granite and rainbow, as she had argued in 'Modern Fiction' and 'Mr Bennett and Mrs Brown' (in which, significantly, Strachey also appeared), so too has the novelist, the modern writer's focus on the mind's infinite effervescent impressions never quite balanced with a depth of solid reality both below and outside it.

What Woolf has in mind is of course a method that will move beyond the boundaries of both genres, an idea first stimulated by her reading of the autobiography of Thomas De Quincey (1785–1859). For his time, she noted there, De Quincey held 'very peculiar views of the art of autobiography', by which he understood 'the history not only of the external life but of the deeper and more hidden emotions' within which 'one moment may transcend in value fifty years' (*CE* IV: 3, 4, 5–6). 'To tell the whole story of a life', Woolf concludes, the writer 'must devise some means by which the two levels of action can be recorded – the rapid passage of events and actions; the slow opening up of single and solemn moments of concentrated emotion' (6).

Woolf's belief in the significance of the intense moment for the revelation of identity bears comparison again with the ideas of Bergson, which given the familiarity of those around her with his theories (including T. S. Eliot, the philosophers Bertrand Russell and Sydney Waterlow, and her sister-in-law Karin Stephen) she would surely have been aware of despite never herself reading his work (*LVW* V: 91). At the end of 'Time and Free Will', Bergson notes that there is an alternative possibility for representing the fundamental self, distinct from both the conventional externalised conception of the ego and the more experimental yet ultimately 'automatic' attempt to transcribe psychic states into language. This 'third course' is 'to carry ourselves back in thought to those moments of our life when we made some serious decision, moments unique of their kind, which will never be repeated'. If such moments, he notes, 'cannot be adequately represented in words or artificially reconstructed by a juxtaposition of simpler states, it is because in their dynamic unity and wholly qualitative multiplicity they are phases of our real and concrete duration' (Bergson, 2001: 239).

It was a method for recovering and articulating such moments of being, as she called them, that Woolf developed in *Mrs Dalloway* (1925), describing it as her 'tunnelling process'.

Like Bergson, Woolf implies that moments of being cannot be straightforwardly narrated, but her constant aim in her fictional writing was to find a way in which their unrepresentable quality might be approximately transcribed, for it is in doing so that she saw the possibility of capturing that elusive element of life: 'making a scene come right; making a character come together' (*MB*: 81). Consider the following passage for example:

Quiet descended on her, calm, content, as her needle, drawing the silk smoothly to its gentle pause, collected the green folds together and attached them, very lightly to the belt. So on a summer's day waves collect, overbalance and fall; collect and fall; and the whole world seems to be saying 'that is all' more and more ponderously, until even the heart in the body which lies in the sun on the beach says too, that is all. Fear no more says the heart. Fear no

> more, says the heart, committing its burden to some sea, which sighs collec-
> tively for all sorrows and renews, begins, collects, lets fall. And the body alone
> listens to the passing bee; the wave breaking, the dog barking, far away barking
> and barking.
>
>   'Heavens, the front-door bell!' exclaimed Clarissa, staying her needle.
> Roused, she listened. (*MD*: 51)

Until the final sentences this passage is not representing what passes through Clarissa's mind, in the manner of *Pilgrimage* or *Ulysses*. Instead Woolf attempts to convey a moment as it is lived in her deep but unformulated consciousness, beneath her otherwise 'tinsely' social personality. This necessitates an impersonal third-person voice separate from that of Clarissa's immediate subjective perceptions, with the role of evoking for the reader that quality of her experience unavailable to her own conscious or semi-conscious awareness, an inner, intuitive and wordless state that she is only barely aware of.

Mrs Dalloway, despite the suggestiveness of its title, nevertheless presents the thoughts and perceptions not of one consciousness but of several, a technique that escapes the singular interior monologues of Joyce and Richardson's fiction to render both the separateness of individual minds but also moments when they interconnect. These interconnections might be framed, at their simplest, by a shared occurrence or spatial environment, such as the aeroplane, the prime minister's car and the chiming of Big Ben that momentarily draw the attention of disparate figures in the city streets, but they are also developed through patterns of common and recurring mental images and phrases that serve to link even characters who never meet, such as Clarissa and the shell-shocked Septimus Smith. This is central to Woolf's method of characterisation, by which a figure is illuminated by the external perceptions of others as much as their own internal consciousness, but also to her conception of identity more generally. Towards the end of the novel, for example, Peter Walsh muses upon Clarissa's theory that 'to know her, or any one, one must seek out the people who completed them' (*MD*: 200). It is in this exploration of the permeability of the self that Woolf's thinking on character and consciousness is perhaps most distinct from that of either Joyce or Richardson.

MULTIPLE SELVES

In Woolf's thinking on character and identity, biography (the story of a life) and autobiography (the story of one's own life) become one. *The Waves* (1931) follows the internal narratives, or 'dramatic soliloquies' (*D* III: 312) as Woolf described them, of six friends, three male and three female, through nine main episodes between infancy and middle-age. Their individual monologues are separate but synchronised, bound together by certain shared mental images and memories that hint at an underlying common pattern to human existence. Moreover, although the voices are typically distinctly personal, inward-looking and self-absorbed, during brief moments the individual limits of consciousness dissolve. In the final section of the novel, for example, Bernard, a writer, attempts to act as the biographer of their different identities, to describe, he says, what 'we call optimistically, "characters of our friends"' (*W*: 204). Yet in so doing he realises that it is his own life that he tells: 'it is not one life that I look back upon; I am not one person; I am many people; I do not altogether know who I am – Jinny, Susan, Neville, Rhoda or Louis: or how to distinguish my life from theirs' (230). Writing of the novel to G. L. Dickinson, Woolf declared, 'I did mean that in some way we are the same person, and not separate people. The six characters were supposed to be one' (*LVW* IV: 397). In this they contrast significantly with the silent Percival, something of a later version of Jacob Flanders and an entirely externalised character, observed through the perceptions of the others. Sports-captain, huntsman and man of Empire, Percival is the representative of conventional literary character, embodying a confident assumption of unified, unreflective selfhood for which Woolf harbours a degree of nostalgia despite rejecting it as obsolete. For the feeling of connection beyond the self in Woolf's writing is always related to the threat of the possible dissolution of that self.

If *Pilgrimage* and *A Portrait of the Artist as a Young Man* are thematically and formally solipsistic in their concentration on the egotistical consciousness, *The Waves* and *Mrs Dalloway* are schizophrenic in their expression of the fragility of the ego. In the former, for example, Neville feels that 'without Percival there is no solidity. We are silhouettes, hollow phantoms moving mistily without a background' (*W*: 100), while Rhoda's connection with an external reality beyond her internal psyche is constantly tenuous. Feeling trapped by the singularity of her physical body she constantly seeks to move beyond it, yet the extreme mental dispersal she consequently experiences places her somewhere between mysticism and madness: 'there is no single scent, no single body for me to follow. And I have no face . . . I am whirled down caverns, and flap like paper against endless corridors, and must press my hand against the wall to draw myself back' (107). Clarissa Dalloway similarly struggles to reconcile the disparity between her private self-image and her public face as Mrs Richard Dalloway, 'her self when some effort, some call on her to be her self, drew the parts together' (*MD*: 47). For Septimus Smith this effort eventually becomes too much, and he ends his life in suicide. Clarissa, hearing of Septimus' death at her party, briefly identifies with him – 'She felt somehow very like him – the young man who had killed himself. She felt glad that he had done it; thrown it away while they went on living' (*MD*: 244) – yet in turn chooses the structure of life over the freedom of death, thinking to herself 'she must go back. She must assemble' (*MD*: 244). For that is life too, Woolf implies, and we are constituted as much by the reflections of others as by our experience of ourselves. In *A Sketch of the Past* she observes:

> This influence, by which I mean the consciousness of other groups impinging upon ourselves; public opinion; what other people say and think; all those magnets which attract us this way to be like that, or repel us the other and make us different from that; has never been analysed in any of those Lives which I so much enjoy reading, or very superficially. Yet it is by such invisible presences that the 'subject of this memoir' is tugged this way and that every day of his life; it is they who keep him in position. (*MB*: 89–90)

Stephen Dedalus and Miriam Henderson make a point of resisting such impingement, but for Woolf's characters it is essential. 'It is Clarissa', Peter Walsh says as Clarissa returns to her guests, 'For there she was' (*MD*: 255).

While the 'psychological' novel was perhaps the most obviously innovative development in the novel in the 1910s and 1920s, it is important to recognise that it had notable detractors even among other consciously experimental writers. D. H. Lawrence, for example, in a series of essays on the modern novel published in 1923 and 1925, attacked the 'absorbedly self-conscious' focus of Joyce, Richardson and Marcel Proust, arguing that their preoccupation with the minutiae of sensation and emotion was both abstract and suffocating (Faulkner, 1986: 135). He advocated that the novel should not focus solely on the internal mind, but instead express 'the whole consciousness in a man, bodily, mental, spiritual at once' (148), in so doing presenting 'new, really new feelings, a whole new line of emotion' that break out of the confines of the individual self to 'a new world *outside*' (137; my italics). Wyndham Lewis similarly regarded the focus of the modern novel on psychological consciousness as a symptom of what he regarded as the widespread malaise of modern Western culture: a self-denying philosophy epitomised by the psychology of Bergson, the physics of Einstein (see Chapter 4) and the literature of Proust, Joyce *and* Lawrence, in which the material was made inferior to the relative and man's rational intellect deemed a lesser power than the vagaries of the unconscious (Lewis, 1993).

SUMMARY

Central to the new realism of the modernist novel was a reconceptualisation of the portrayal of character and identity, and a preoccupation with how to represent the mind's surface consciousness and unconscious depths in narrative. For as psychological and philosophical theory demonstrated the significance of mental phenomena such as dreams, instinctive associations and memories, and confidence in the reliability of external or surface appearance dissolved, writers were faced with the challenge of conveying both the multiple, transient perceptions of the individual self on the one hand, and a profound sense of the irrevocable strangeness of another human being on the other. Joyce, Woolf and Richardson's strategies for doing so is often referred to as 'stream of consciousness', a metaphor used originally to describe the way thoughts flow in the mind, but quickly appropriated as a term for the literary technique that attempts to translate them into narrative form. Their technical innovations in the narration of the human consciousness were yet nuanced and varied. In terms of style their novels include a range of modes of internal narrative, from those that do not diverge greatly from the organisation and syntax of ordinary speech (as in Woolf's novels, much of *Pilgrimage* and *A Portrait of the Artist as a Young Man*), to the less formal rendering of thought or sensory impressions (as in other parts of *Pilgrimage* and the first half of *Ulysses*). In terms of focus only Richardson concentrated her entire body of writing through a single (autobiographical) subjective consciousness. In the later episodes of *Ulysses* Joyce largely departs from interior monologue, and in *Finnegans Wake* dispenses with it entirely. Speculating more on the multiple and collective rather than individualising aspects of identity, Woolf's writing weaves in and out of different consciousnesses that momentarily overlap or intertwine. Concerned with how to grasp and communicate a quality of existence that she argued must lie beneath the surface consciousness of the mind, and that connected human lives across the self-contained limits of individual subjective experience, it is this persistent preoccupation with the dispersed, non-bounded nature of the self and mind that perhaps most distinguishes her portrayal of character from the strategies of either Richardson or Joyce.

3

GENDER AND THE
NOVEL

In a review for the *Times Literary Supplement* in 1920, Virginia Woolf quoted the words of Bathsheba Everdene in Thomas Hardy's *Far From the Madding Crowd* as exemplifying the position of women as both subjects and writers of the English novel: 'I have the feelings of a woman, but I have only the language of men' (*E* II: 67). Even with the growing emancipation of women in the twentieth century, Woolf notes, the difficulty for a woman of speaking in her own voice remains:

> From that dilemma arise infinite confusions and complications. Energy has been liberated, but into what forms is it to flow? To try the accepted forms, to discard the unfit, to create others which are more fitting, is a task that must be accomplished before there is freedom or achievement. (67)

Nine years later the relation of women and fiction, and in particular the social and ideological conditions that have impeded women from writing, became the focus of her pioneering study in feminist literary criticism, *A Room of One's Own* (1929). Dorothy Richardson's thinking on the socially and historically conditioned relation of women and fiction (her resentment at the definitions of femininity by male writers, her rage at the complicity of women in a culture that prioritises the lives of men, and her understanding of the social and economic obstacles facing the woman writer), articulated in both *Pilgrimage* and a series of articles on women and feminism in the early 1920s, noticeably pre-empts Woolf's similar arguments in *A Room of One's Own*. In her attempt to evolve a form of literature appropriate to the expression of a 'female' voice, however, she ultimately diverges from Woolf, who imagined the possibility of moving beyond gender categories, advocating an androgynous literary aesthetic that would represent neither a specifically masculine nor specifically feminine point of view. The implicit dialogue between Woolf and Richardson in the 1920s over the gendered nature of literary style was given additional context by the association of a so-called 'feminine sentence' with the 'stream-of-consciousness' narrative focus of the modernist novel more generally, irrespective of the actual sex of the writer or protagonist. For both women writers James Joyce became a figure whose purportedly 'feminine' prose in *Ulysses* they needed to distinguish carefully from their own 'women's' writing.

A ROOM OF ONE'S OWN

Woolf's *A Room of One's Own* is arguably *the* founding text of twentieth-century feminist literary criticism, and along with her essays 'Women and Fiction' and 'Professions for Woman', which take up similar themes, forms the core of her thinking on the relationship of women and fiction. The starting premise of her argument in all three is a fundamentally material one: 'a woman must have money and a room of her own if she is to write fiction' (*AROO*: 4). The demands of the domestic household, the laws that denied married women ownership of funds or property, and a lack of educational opportunity, made it almost impossible for a woman before the nineteenth century to take up writing as a profession. Writing requires time, privacy and literacy, and women suffered from too little of all of these things. Woolf then elaborates a range of theories – about the exclusion of women from literary history, the construction of 'femininity' within patriarchal discourse, the importance of a tradition or heritage of women's writing, the relation of sex and genre, and the gendered qualities of literary style – which pre-empt many of those taken up in more recent cultural and literary analysis. Anxious that her polemical argument for women's financial and social independence from men would provoke a negative response among the largely male critical institution, she awaited reviews with considerable nervousness: 'I shall be attacked for a feminist and hinted at for a Sapphist', she noted in her diary, 'I am afraid it will not be taken seriously' (*D* III: 262).

Central to Woolf's feminist literary criticism is her belief that literature is always based in its historical moment, 'like a spider's web, attached ever so lightly perhaps, but still attached to life at all four corners' (*AROO*: 53). We have already seen her make this argument in both her 'Modern Fiction' and 'Mr Bennett and Mrs Brown' essays, in which she suggests that modern times require and influence a new focus and form of writing on the part of the modern writer. Now this is directed specifically at women's writing, as Woolf considers the effects of women's social situation on their writing (and lack of) at different periods in history. By 'life', moreover, she asserts that she means 'grossly material things, like health and money and the houses we live in' (54). Women's economic, social and political powerlessness, she notes, has resulted in centuries of cultural representation that privilege things regarded as important by men, and that have consequently marginalised female experience. History books, for example, concentrate on the 'great movements' of government, empire or scientific revolution that make up 'the historian's view of the past' (57–8), and which are dominated by the actions and values of men:

> His was the power and the money and the influence. He was the proprietor of the paper and its editor and sub-editor. He was the Foreign Secretary and the Judge. He was the cricketer; he owned the racehorses and the yachts. He was the director of the company that pays two hundred per cent to its shareholders. He left millions to charities and colleges that were ruled by himself. (43)

If historical narrative ignores women, fiction has mythologised them in a manner that bears little relation to reality. 'Some of the most inspired words, some of the most profound thoughts in literature fall from her lips', she observes drily of women in the age of Shakespeare, but 'in real life she could hardly read, could scarcely spell, and was the property of her husband' (56). It is hardly surprising, she asserts, that women writers play little part in literary history prior to the nineteenth century. The creative voice of even the most gifted women would have remained mute, through want of support, education and opportunity.

The image of woman that emerges from this combination of historical indifference and imaginative fascination on the part of male writers, Woolf argues, has constituted no less of a difficulty for the potential woman writer than the practical difficulties of time and money. For she is faced not only with the practical difficulties preventing her from writing, but also the influential yet false image of female identity established by the male-oriented ethos of Western culture and society.

Man's self-confidence, Woolf argues, depends on his sense of power and superiority. The idolised Angel of the House nurtures that self-confidence. When women refuse their culturally assigned domestic role, however, assert their own independence and dare to criticise male psychology and ways of life, as by the end of the nineteenth century they were beginning to do, he responds with angry panic. 'Women have served all these centuries as looking-glasses possessing the magic and delicious power of reflecting the figure of man at twice its natural size', Woolf notes, but 'if she begins to tell the truth, the figure in the looking-glass shrinks; his fitness for life is diminished' (*AROO*: 45, 46). Recalling the intensity with which a respected male friend described the writer Rebecca West as an 'arrant feminist!', for example, Woolf recognises: 'it was a protest against some infringement of his power to believe in himself' (45). This in part explains, she thinks, the number of quasi-scientific books recently written about women by men (her references to 'Freudian theory', 'psycho-analysis' and 'Fiji islanders' suggest that she has both psychological and anthropological theories in mind here), all preoccupied with demonstrating 'the mental, moral and physical inferiority of women' (41). All these books, she decides, are not really concerned with women at all, but rather with the reassertion of the superiority of men at a moment when women were calling for emancipation.

Dorothy Richardson had made a similar point a decade previously, representing the young Miriam Henderson's angry frustration at the cultural construction of women in all of her reading as the inferior helpmates of men. In *The Tunnel* (1919), for example, she is horrified by the 'loathsome images' of contemporary science, in which the female species is presented as 'inferior, mentally, morally, intellectually and physically' (*P*

THE ANGEL OF THE HOUSE

Woolf's concept of the 'angel of the house' refers to a popular nineteenth-century poem of the same name by Coventry Patmore, which eulogises the influential Victorian ideal of deferential, supportive and domestic womanhood. In 'Professions for Women' Woolf cites this figure as the main obstacle facing the woman writer in the nineteenth century. During her childhood, she notes, 'every house had its angel':

> She was intensely sympathetic. She was immensely charming. She was utterly unselfish. She excelled in the difficult arts of family life. She sacrificed herself daily. If there was chicken, she took the leg; if there was a draught she sat in it – in short she was so constituted that she never had a mind or a wish of her own, but preferred to sympathize always with the minds and wishes of others. Above all – I need not say it – she was pure. Her purity was supposed to be her chief beauty – her blushes, her great grace. (*WW*: 59)

The strength of this cultural myth, Woolf states, internalised by women themselves, was a more subtle yet no less formidable impediment to women's self-expression than their lack of financial independence, and one of the main obstacles that she had faced when starting out as a writer. For Woolf the 'angel' becomes a 'phantom', who appears when she begins to write and tries to control the opinions of her pen. To kill the angel of the house, she declares, was crucial to the profession of a woman writer:

> Had I not killed her she would have killed me. She would have plucked the heart out of my writing. For, as I found, directly I put pen to paper, you cannot review even a novel without having a mind of your own, without expressing what you think to be the truth about human relations, morality, sex. And all these questions, according to the Angel of the House, cannot be dealt with freely and openly by women. (*WW*: 59)

II: 220), and finds in the alternative of religion 'nothing but insults for women' (222). '*How* could Newnham and Girton women endure it?', Miriam asks herself, '[a]ll books were poisoned. All life was poisoned, for women, at the very essence' (219, 220). Women's own collusion in such male definitions of life and reality, Miriam finds an act of betrayal. In her previous life, she remembers in *Backwater* (1916), when she had read the blissful depictions of 'angel of the house'-type married harmony in the works of Rosa Nouchette Carey and Mrs Hungerford, 'it had seemed quite possible that life might suddenly develop into the thing the writer described' (*P* I: 284). In the initial bewilderment, disillusionment and shame of her working life, however, she can no longer connect herself with such romantic images – 'these things could only happen to people with money. She would never have even the smallest share of that sort of life' (285). By supporting this myth of idyllic domesticity, she realises moreover, women stifle their own individual identity: 'What an escape! Good god in heaven, what an escape! Far better to be alone and suffering and miserable here in the school, alive' (284). It is this conscious self-dis-avowal that accounts for Miriam's frequent outbursts of hatred towards women, which, as with Woolf's killing of her phantom angel, are far more violent than her typical response to men.

Miriam's room of her own, the four grey walls in the Tansley Street boarding house that witness the struggles of her London life, is hard won and for all the independence that it offers comes at a cost. 'Art demands what, to women, current civilization won't give', Richardson declared in an essay on 'Women in the Arts' in 1925, freedom not only from the practical responsibilities of women's lives but also from 'the human demand, besieging her wherever she is, for an inclusive awareness, from which men, for good or ill, are exempt' (Kime Scott, 1990: 423). Every household, every friendship and relationship, Richardson implies, requires a degree of emotional commitment and attention on the part of women that is greater than that of men (an argument that follows from her belief that the male and female psyches are essentially different, as we will go on to explore below). In *Pilgrimage* Miriam Henderson struggles constantly against the demands of work, friendships and relationships, reaching the point of breakdown before she decides that she must detach herself from all of them in order fully to realise her individual autonomy.

Despite the element of idealism in Woolf's discussion of the room of one's own, she nevertheless did not underestimate the difficulties women faced in achieving economic independence. While she herself came from a wealthy family, the denial of the university education afforded her brothers and stepbrothers, and the knowledge of being beholden to finan-cial handouts from her father, made her fully aware of the patriarchal bias of intellectual and economic power. Yet she was well aware that women's work (largely clerical) was hard and poorly paid, and in itself not conducive to suitable conditions for writing. Five hundred pounds a year, she suggests in both *A Room of One's Own* and 'Professions for Women', was the amount of money required for a woman in the early twentieth century to have the financial independence that would allow her to free herself from the expected cultural role of the Angel of the House. If a woman could make that money herself, through her own pen, then she could begin to write as she wished, in her own voice.

A FEMALE LITERARY HERITAGE

Woolf herself, however, warned against the assumption that a woman's financial independence was *all* that was needed for her to write. It may seem that once a woman had achieved a room of her own and refused the cultural expectations of her domestic role, she 'had only to be herself', she notes in 'Professions for Women', 'but what is "herself"? I mean, what is a woman?' (*WW*: 60). Writing as a woman, Woolf tells her audience, 'telling the truth about my own experiences as a body' (62), was something she did not think she or any other writer had yet achieved.

One of the reasons for the difficulty women writers have in speaking truthfully of their own experiences and developing their own forms of expression, Woolf argues in *A Room of One's Own*, is the lack of a tradition of female literature to draw on for example. In her own reviews she frequently argued for the importance of a female literary heritage in influencing the work of subsequent women writers, and set out to recover a legacy of female creative expression from the exclusionary male-focussed narratives of canonical literary history.

The most significant moment in the history of women's fiction, Woolf declares, came with the eighteenth century when middle-class women first began to write as a profession. Before this time, she notes, only a few aristocratic women had been able to indulge a passion for writing, their wealth and position allowing them to learn both to read and write and, in some cases, to ignore the ridicule of society. This changed, however, when Aphra Behn (1640–89), widowed at the age of twenty-six, took up the pen in order to support herself and became the first *professional* woman

TRADITION

Woolf's discussion of a female literary heritage compares interestingly with T. S. Eliot's idea of artistic tradition in his essay 'Tradition and the Individual Talent' (1919). According to Eliot, every work of art is attributed value and meaning through contrast or comparison with every other, forming a literary order (or 'tradition'), the proportional relations of which are constantly readjusted as new works are created. It is the responsibility of the writer, Eliot asserts, to be aware of the historical and aesthetic significance of his own work in relation to the great literature and writers of the past. Woolf draws attention to the gendered bias of this tradition, literary history having long been dominated by the names of male writers and the standards of male critics. In *A Room of One's Own* she asserts that 'we think back through our mothers if we are women' (*AROO*: 99), and in 'Professions for Women' claims that her own career was made possible because 'many famous women, and many more unknown and forgotten, have been before me, making the path smooth, and regulating my steps' (*WW*: 57). Woolf's feminist ideals were not always compatible with her literary critical judgements however, and while many of her essays concentrate on reclaiming the *historical* significance of past women writers, in others the key *aesthetic* and more contemporary influences on her writing are clearly male (Dostoevsky, James, Proust).

dramatist and novelist. Raising the status of women's fiction from a merely frivolous pastime to a skilled occupation, perhaps even more importantly for Woolf she showed that writing could provide a means to women's financial independence. Given Behn's colourful reputation it is unlikely that women suddenly flocked to writing in the droves that Woolf's rhetoric somewhat suggests, but certainly she led the way for the development of women's fiction as a profession in the eighteenth century. Much of that writing, Woolf admits, was probably very bad and has largely been forgotten. Nevertheless, she argues, whatever their various quality the voices of these many women formed a chorus that made possible the masterpieces of the few:

> Without those forerunners, Jane Austen and the Brontës and George Eliot could no more have written than Shakespeare could have written without Marlowe, or Marlowe without Chaucer, or Chaucer without those forgotten poets who paved

the ways and tamed the natural savagery of the tongue. For masterpieces are not single and solitary births; they are the outcome of many years of thinking in common, of thinking by the body of the people, so that the experience of the mass is behind the single voice. (*AROO*: 91)

Woolf here constructs a lineage of women writers whose collective legacy supports and nurtures the writing of those who follow, and in which famous names are no more or less significant than those that have been lost.

By the nineteenth century, women writers were prominent participants within the literary scene, notably, Woolf observes with curiosity, in the genre of the novel. In practical terms the novel was a rapidly expanding popular market that paid consistently and well (see also Showalter, 1977; Spencer, 1986), but Woolf suggests that it was also the genre most amenable to women's circumstances and most suited to the expression of their experience; it only required a pencil and paper, it dealt in the everyday life and emotions that typically constituted women's lives, and could be written in the brief interludes between domestic and

SHAKESPEARE'S SISTER

Arguing that the lack of a great woman poet to rival Shakespeare is the result of social inequality rather than any lack of creative capacity on women's part, Woolf imagines what would have been the fate of Shakespeare's sister, if he had one and if, equally artistic, she had tried to make a career for herself in the theatre. When Judith Shakespeare runs away to London, she is met with ridicule and refused employment. Seduced and abandoned, she ends up committing suicide before she has a chance to write a word. In direct comparison to the concept of the 'Angel of the House', the phantom of Victorian womanhood that Woolf identified as haunting every prospective woman writer, the spirit of 'Shakespeare's sister' yet exists as a latent yet stimulating force, awaiting the opportunity to be reborn. Woolf closes *A Room of One's Own* by urging her female readers to take full advantage of their own social and economic freedom, in order to bring about a world in which this creative female spirit 'shall find it possible to live and write her poetry' (149).

social duties. As she begins to consider the beginnings of the women's novel, however, it becomes increasingly clear that the material obstacles that faced women as writers formed the basis for further cultural, psychological and aesthetic ones.

The woman writer in the nineteenth century, Woolf argues, was conscious that her work would be assessed according to the cultural expectations of her gender, and pronounced sentimental or monstrous accordingly. She thus wrote with a mixture of fear and anger, 'admitting that she was "only a woman", or protesting that she was "as good as a man"' (*AROO*: 96). At a basic level this can be seen in women writers' use of marital status (Mrs Gaskell) or male pseudonyms (Currer Bell, George Eliot) for publishing purposes. Yet this internalisation of gender stereotypes, Woolf argues, also compromised the woman writer's artistic vision. It is complete faithfulness to this vision, which she refers to as 'integrity', that allows the novelist to bring together life and art and capture a sense of reality. That integrity is lost, however, when the writer allows her personal feelings to intrude upon her work. The majority of novels by women in the nineteenth century fail to convince, she suggests, because their artistic integrity is fundamentally flawed; the writer's creative voice is either subdued in deference to male authority, or overwhelmed by resentment against it. Thus Charlotte Brontë, for example, is accused of allowing passages of personal anger to intrude upon *Jane Eyre*:

> if one reads them over and marks that jerk in them, that indignation, one sees that she will never get her genius expressed whole and entire. Her books will be deformed and twisted. She will write in a rage where she should write calmly. She will write foolishly where she should write wisely. She will write of herself when she should write of her characters. (90)

Similarly she argues that Elizabeth Barrett Browning, in writing *Aurora Leigh*, 'could no more conceal herself than she could control herself, a sign no doubt of imperfection in an artist, but a sign also that life has impinged upon art more than life should' (*WW*: 137). Even George Eliot, Woolf suggests, cannot suppress her frustration and discontent at her own womanhood, becoming in the representation of her female characters 'self-conscious, didactic, and occasionally vulgar' (157). The result in the work of all these and many other writers besides, she argues in 'Women and Fiction', is that '[t]he vision becomes too masculine or it becomes too feminine; it loses its perfect integrity and, with that, its most essential quality as a work of art' (48). Only Jane Austen is credited with the ability to ignore both the idealisation and the criticism of her sex, as well as through a perspective of ironic detachment to write without her artistic integrity warped by the weight of shame or resentment at her status as a woman.

Given her ostensible purpose of rediscovering a tradition of women's writing, Woolf's attack on the Victorian female canon of Brontë, Eliot and Barrett Browning might seem surprising. It has certainly been met with resistance by some feminist literary critics, for whom the Victorian writers' explicit articulation of and rebellion against their sex involves far greater female solidarity than what they regard as Woolf's introverted focus on the individual subjective consciousness and her espousal of an aesthetic of androgyny (Showalter, 1977). It is a response, as we will go on to explore further in the final chapter, arising out of the critical perspective that pits the supposed social engagement of realism against the elitism and social detachment of modernism. Woolf's critical estimation of Austen as 'the most perfect artist among women' and 'the forerunner of Henry James and of Proust' (*WW*: 120) is based in her approval of the latter's controlled artistry and narrative impersonality, qualities which accord with her modernist principles. It is worth keeping in mind that although Woolf describes Austen as writing as a *woman*, she implies that she is able to do so because she writes primarily as an *artist*.

FEMININE SENTENCES

The consideration of a 'female' literary style dominates Woolf's discussion of contemporary women's fiction in *A Room of One's Own*. Previously, she argues, women writers have only had available to them the language of men. Only in the twentieth century, she suggests, has the woman writer begun to mould 'a prose style completely expressive of her mind' (*AROO*: 124). Far from making a new argument, however, Woolf was here summarising a broad and vigorous debate over the concept and practice of 'feminine' prose within which she had participated almost a decade earlier.

One of Woolf's first contributions for the *TLS* was a review of W. L. Courtney's *The Feminine Note in Fiction* in 1905, in which she queried whether it was 'not too soon . . . to criticise the "feminine note" in anything?' (*E* I: 15). By the publication of R. Brimley Johnson's *Some Contemporary Novelists (Women)*, however, devoted to fourteen modern writers (including Richardson and Woolf), a shift in the focus and form of women's literature was becoming more apparent, characterised above all by a concern with the exploration of female consciousness:

> the new woman, the feminine novelist of the twentieth century, has abandoned the old realism. She does not accept observed revelation. She is seeking with passionate determination for that Reality which is behind the material, the things that matter, spiritual things, ultimate Truth. And here she finds man an outsider, wilfully blind, purposefully indifferent. (Brimley Johnson, 1920: xiv–xv)

The basic terms of Brimley Johnson's analysis (an old, social and material realism versus a new, egoistic and spiritual one) are familiar to us from Woolf's 'Modern Novels' and 'Modern Fiction' essays, but what is distinctive here is his suggestion that this divide was also a gendered one, in which the 'new' realism is associated with a specifically female literary voice. The writer whom he argued provided the 'most extreme and consistent' and 'most original' example of the new feminine realism was Dorothy Richardson, who by 1920 was already almost at the peak of her recognition as the pioneer of an innovative and influential method of writing and an assertively individualist feminism.

There is no indication that Woolf read Brimley Johnson's book, possibly out of anxiety that professional rivalry would cloud her critical judgement, as she had accused Katherine Mansfield of doing in her review of *Night and Day* less than a year before. However, she *had* reviewed its prequel on eighteenth- and nineteenth-century women realist novelists for the *TLS* two years previously, declaring that Johnson, 'besides saying some very interesting things about literature, . . . says also many that are even more interesting about the peculiar qualities of the literature that is written by women' (*WW*: 68). Woolf calls attention, as we might by now expect, to the social and ideological conditions that influence those qualities, but ultimately seems to agree with Johnson's argument that the form and focus of women's fiction is distinct from that of men, noting the significance of 'the difference between the man's and the woman's view of what constitutes the importance of any subject', from which 'spring not only marked differences of plot and incident, but infinite differences in selection, method and style' (71). It was exactly such differences that Johnson went on to elaborate in his study of new realist women writers, and that Richardson's conception of producing a 'feminine equivalent' to masculine realism epitomised. In *A Room of One's Own*, however, Richardson and her contemporaries are conspicuous by their absence. Following the wealth of real literary figures that fill the first two-thirds of the essay, when Woolf reaches the development of women's prose in the twentieth century she turns instead to a *hypothetical* example: a first novel by the imaginary Mary Carmichael. Her account yet strikingly resembles the two reviews she did write on Richardson's *The Tunnel* and *Revolving Lights*. Mary Carmichael, she tells the reader in *A Room of One's Own*, writes predominantly about women in relation to other women rather than to men, experiments with the flow of the sentence and the chronological sequence of the narrative, and possesses a sensibility that is 'very wide, eager, and free', alert to 'every sight and sound that came its way' (121). Compare this with her account of *The Tunnel* in 1919, where she states:

> it represents a genuine conviction of the discrepancy between what she has to say and the form provided by tradition for her to say it in. . . . 'him and her' are cut out, and with them goes the odd deliberate business: the chapters that lead up and the chapters that lead down; the characters who are always characteristic; . . . All these things are cast away, and there is left, denuded, unsheltered, unbegun and unfinished, the consciousness of Miriam Henderson, the small sensitive lump of matter, half transparent and half opaque, which endlessly reflects. (*E* III: 10)

Moving on we find that Mary Carmichael is described as writing 'as a woman, but as a woman who has forgotten that she is a woman, so that her pages were full of that curious sexual quality which comes only when sex is unconscious of itself' (*AROO*: 121). Likewise, writing on *Revolving Lights* in 1923, Woolf had credited Richardson with developing a mode of writing that was able to depict the depths of the female psyche, and was not distorted by any sense of a need to justify that psyche:

> She has invented, or, if she has not invented, developed and applied to her own uses, a sentence which we might call the psychological sentence of the feminine gender. It is of a more elastic fibre than the old, capable of stretching to the extreme, of suspending the frailest particles, of enveloping the vaguest shapes. Other writers of the opposite sex have used sentences of this description and stretched them to the extreme. But there is a difference. Miss Richardson has fashioned her sentence consciously, in order that it may descend to the depths and investigate the crannies of Miriam Henderson's consciousness. It is a woman's sentence, but only in the sense that it is used to describe a woman's mind by a writer who is neither proud nor afraid of anything that she may discover in the psychology of her own sex. (*E* III: 367)

Woolf's last point here is ambiguous when set apart from the context of *A Room of One's Own*: is she commending Richardson's type of woman's sentence or suggesting it has limitations? From the evidence of her account of the writing of Mary Carmichael, it would seem that she means the former. Both real and imaginary writer consciously evolve a literary style that expresses a woman's mind objectively, avoiding the personal bitterness or defensiveness that she thought marred the work of Eliot or the Brontës. It is a style – the 'psychological sentence of the feminine gender' – that is not exclusive to the woman writer or even to the representation of female consciousness, but it is distinguishable in Richardson's work because it is used to portray a *woman's* mind, and therefore becomes in its focus and subject-matter a specifically 'woman's sentence'.

The concept of a style and form of literary expression specific to women is something that Woolf contemplates with considerable ambiguity. At the end of Chapter 4 in *A Room of One's Own* she argues that the standard form and sentence of the nineteenth-century novel was 'unsuited for a woman's use'. It was 'a man's sentence', she observes, 'behind it one can see Johnson, Gibbon and the rest' (*AROO*: 100). Referring here to Samuel Johnson (1709–84), who wrote the first English dictionary, and Edward Gibbon (1737–94), the first modern historian and author of the mammoth *History of the Decline and Fall of the Roman Empire*, she is associating both the founding rules and principles of linguistic meaning and the the-matic focus of historical narrative with the interests of men. Woolf's defi-nition of a 'woman's sentence' we might therefore assume to be based in the development of a new style of language and a new focus in theme and subject-matter that would be specific to women; something that might look very much like the 'stream-of-consciousness' style narrative of lit-erary modernism. Her claim, however, that Jane Austen 'devised a per-fectly natural, shapely sentence for her own use' (100) makes it clear that she does *not* regard a 'woman's' sentence as being necessarily avant-garde in style. Her thinking at this point is further complicated by her sugges-tion that a novel 'has somehow to be adapted to the body', and that as a result 'women's books should be shorter, more concentrated, than those of men' (101), because domestic demands present them with less avail-able time in which to write. Here Woolf's initial social and material argu-ment about the characteristics of women's writing is linked to what appears to be a biological conception of the relation of literature and sexual difference. Her reference to the body, however, remains firmly grounded within her discussion of a writer's social context, refusing a reductive relation of the sex of a writer and literary form.

While Woolf attempted to move beyond the gendered ideology of patriarchal thought, she yet retained a faith in the real social and physical differences between men's and women's lives. This is where the concept of the woman's sentence plays an important role in Woolf's thinking. The woman's sentence is defined by its *subject-matter* rather than its form, and can only be written by a woman because that subject-matter is based in a woman's social, psychological and historical experience. That experi-ence will alter at different periods (remember Woolf's insistence on the influence of social and historical context on a writer's work) and the style and form of the writing will alter accordingly, but it will remain funda-mentally a 'woman's' sentence by virtue of being written out of a woman's life and being. What we return to here is her assertion in 'Woman Novelists' that it is impossible to mistake a novel written by a man for one written by a woman, an argument that is reiterated in her distinction of Richardson's 'woman's' sentence, which depicts a woman's mind, from the experimental 'feminine sentence' used by her male con-temporaries.

THE SENTENCE OF FEMININE GENDER

The 'feminine' sentence and the 'woman's' sentence are different kinds of categories for thinking about fiction. What Woolf refers to when she speaks of the former is a particular *style* of writing – psychological in focus, innovative in technique – that might be described as 'feminine' by virtue of its opposing dominant 'masculine' ideology (of which materialist literary realism was a part) but that could be written by either a man or a woman. It is an idea that anticipates the concept of 'patriarchal binary thought' in later post-structuralist theory, which argues that systems of thought and meaning in dominant society operate according to a series of hierarchical oppositions in which the stronger is always defined as a 'masculine' characteristic and the weaker as 'feminine'. To describe literary style as 'feminine' in this sense is to accord it qualities that are the opposite of those which society conventionally designates as 'masculine'. While this could take the form of an intentionally radical and positive move, in which the intention is to reverse the dominant ideological hierarchy, the problem is that perpetuating the basic oppositional structure of binary thought naturalises the identification of women with the culturally ascribed 'weaker' characteristics of the 'feminine'. And of course more often than not those characteristics are applied negatively (see Wyndham Lewis' critique of Joyce in *Time and Western Man* for just such an example). For a summary of subsequent debate within feminist and post-structuralist literary criticism on the concept of 'feminine' writing and its relation to avant-garde literary style, see Cixous, 1968; Gilbert and Gubar, 1985; Moi, 1985; Kime Scott, 1987; Henke, 1990.

THE ETERNAL FEMININE AND THE WOMANLY WOMAN

The representation of femininity in Joyce's writings is notoriously ambiguous, capable of supporting both those critics who accuse him of misogynistically perpetuating the social stereotypes of Mother, Virgin and Whore that reduce women to the body (Gilbert and Gubar, 1985), and those who celebrate him for identifying femininity with a textual and linguistic errancy that undercuts the patriarchal social order (see also Lawrence, 1990). Both arguments typically focus on the 'Penelope' section of *Ulysses*, which presents the internal consciousness of the semi-awake Molly Bloom, her fleshly memories and sensations, and half-formed, merging thoughts and associations presented in only eight sentences. One of Joyce's longest and most quoted explanations of the episode was to Frank Budgen in 1921, in which he announced, '*Penelope* is the clou of the book':

> The first sentence contains 2500 words. There are eight sentences in the episode. It begins and ends with the female word *yes*. It turns like the huge earth ball slowly surely and evenly round and round spinning, its four cardinal points being the female breasts, arse, womb and cunt expressed by the words *because, bottom* (in all senses bottom button, bottom of the class, bottom of the sea, bottom of his heart), *woman, yes*. Though probably more obscene than any preceding episode it seems to me to be perfectly sane full amoral fertilisable untrustworthy engaging shrewd limited prudent indifferent *Weib. Ich bin der Fleisch der stets bejaht.* ['*Woman. I am the flesh that always affirms*'] (*LJJ* I: 169)

'Penelope' here is imagined as the narrative of archetypal, eternal 'Woman', defined by her reproductive body rather than her mind, and identified with Nature and the earth. Note, however, that Joyce warns that it is also 'untrustworthy' and 'indifferent', a point reiterated in 'Calypso' when Bloom observes exasperatedly of Molly's thought processes that, 'She followed not all, a part of the whole, gave attention with interest, comprehended with surprise, with care repeated, with greater difficulty remembered, forgot with ease, with misgiving reremembered, rerepeated with error' (*U*: 804). In writing Molly's narrative Joyce was recycling, but also exposing and satirising normative cultural constructions of womanliness and female consciousness, just as he had similarly done with other social and cultural discourses and ideologies in each of the previous episodes of the novel. Yet in addition he was also writing a coda to the novel as a whole, offering what he described as an 'indispensable countersign' to all that had gone before it (*LJJ* I: 160). For while the ignorance, guile, contradictoriness, narcissism and triviality that characterise the subject-matter of Molly's internal monologue conform to a conventional stereotype of the female mind, her narrative unreliability and disregard for logical thinking could also be seen to represent an alternative to the formal structures of patriarchal thought that produces such stereotypes.

Virginia Woolf's reference to the elasticity of the psychological sentence of the feminine gender in her review of Richardson's *Revolving Lights* of course repeats her description of Joyce's writing in 'Modern Novels', and *Ulysses* is certainly one of the examples she has in mind when she refers to it being stretched to its extreme by male writers. In translating a supposedly womanly bodily consciousness in 'Penelope', however, Joyce stretches the 'feminine' sentence even further, audaciously presuming to give voice to exactly that truth about woman's lives as bodies that Woolf refers to in 'Professions for Women': to write, in other words, not only a 'feminine' but a 'woman's' sentence. Joyce was extremely curious about what he regarded as the unspoken or secret language of women. Despite his averred hostility towards psychoanalysis he often wrote down interpretations of his wife's dreams. In the 'Calypso' section of *Ulysses*, Bloom imagines using fragments of Molly's speech to write a story:

> Might manage a sketch. By Mr and Mrs L. M. Bloom. Invent a story for some proverb. Which? Time I used to try jotting down on my cuff what she said dressing. (*U*: 84)

Molly in turn thinks similarly in 'Penelope': 'if I only could remember the I half of the things and write a book out of it the works of Master Poldy yes' (893). The notation of Molly's narrative, moreover, with its long merging sentences and lack of punctuation, owed much to Joyce's interest in the fact that both Nora and his aunt Josephine regularly ignored full stops and capitals when writing letters (*LJJ* II: 173). Dorothy Richardson later identified irregular punctuation as a characteristic of women's natural way of writing (for her it indicated the multiplicity and unbounded quality of female consciousness), noting that it was a *stylistic* aspect of 'feminine prose' of which Joyce had 'delightfully shown [himself] to be aware' (Kime Scott, 1990: 396).

Joyce's fascination with the possibility of gaining access to the private life of women is evident as early as his essay on Ibsen, of whose female characters he declared: 'he seems to know them better than they know themselves. Indeed, if one may say so of an eminently virile man, there is a curious admixture of the woman in his nature. His marvellous accuracy, his faint traces of femininity, his delicacy of swift touch, are perhaps attributable to this admixture. But that he knows women is an uncontrovertible fact' (*OCP*: 45–6). It is a statement that looks forward to both the figure of Leopold Bloom, 'the new womanly man' (*U*: 614), and, as with many of Joyce's descriptions of Ibsen, elements of his own self as a mature artist. The psychoanalyst Carl Jung, for example, declared after reading *Ulysses* that he had not known so much about 'the real psychology of a woman' (Ellmann, 1982: 629). Yet while the young Joyce could confidently assert that a male writer could fully understand women, the older artist was uncharacteristically more modest. He told several friends of a dream in which he carefully explained the meaning of the 'Penelope' episode to Molly Bloom herself, only for her to rebuke him angrily for 'meddling' with her 'business' (Ellmann, 1982: 549). In one of the many self-reflexive references to *Ulysses* in *Finnegans Wake*, moreover, he admits that, however much he may have affected Molly's internal voice, her narrative is nevertheless the work of a male hand, in which 'the penelopean patience of its last paraphe' with its representation of the 'vaulting feminine libido of those interbranching ogham sex upandinsweeps' is yet ultimately 'sternly controlled and easily repersuaded by the uniform matteroffactness of a meandering male fist' (*FW*: 123). Both novels are purportedly drawn to open-ends in flowing, 'female' soliloquy – Molly's welcoming 'Yes' and ALP's dying sentence, which tails off only to begin the whole novel again – but in each it is the author who has the last word, signing off the completion of his work: 'Trieste-Zürich-Paris, 1914–21' (*U*: 933), 'PARIS, 1922–39' (*FW*: 628).

Richardson's belief in the basic and insurmountable difference between the male and female psyche, and her redefinition of the ways in which masculine society has conceived that difference, is central to understanding her representation of feminine consciousness as the crucial concern of both the form and focus of *Pilgrimage*. If the purpose of the novel was to articulate exactly the secret voice of women separate from the framing interpretations of male culture and language that Joyce was interested in, however, the manner of that voice was very different. For all the critical comparisons of Joyce and Richardson's formal rendering of female interior monologue, Molly Bloom and Miriam Henderson are two of the most profoundly dissimilar women characters in modernist literature: the 'stream of consciousness' of the former instinctive, passive and earthily physical, that of the latter self-conscious, individualist and hyper-sensitively aware. Molly's role, despite the prosaic details that fill her thoughts, was to represent archetypal 'Woman'; her narrative is conceived out of male notions of femininity, albeit acknowledged by Joyce himself. Miriam's role was to refuse masculine stereotypes both of women but also of thought and experience more generally, with the conscious objective of living in faithfulness to her individual female consciousness.

Richardson had outlined her definition of male and female difference in a review article 'The Reality of Feminism' in 1917, contrasting the classificatory, formulaic tendency of the male mind with what she considered to be the integrated, synthesising quality of female consciousness, arguing for '[a] fearless constructive feminism [that] will re-read the past in the light of its present recognition of the synthetic consciousness of woman; will recognise that this consciousness has always made its own world, irrespective of circumstances' (Kime Scott, 1990: 406). Woman, she notes, 'is relatively to man, *synthetic*. Men tend to fix life, to fix aspects. They create metaphysical systems, religions, arts, and sciences. Woman *is* metaphysical, religious, an artist and scientist in life' (404; my italics). This distinction between a masculine rational mentality and feminine intuitive being recalls Henri Bergson's similar but ungendered theory of consciousness noted in Chapter 2. Man's understanding and way of being in the world is based in an externalised and compartmentalised relation to reality, whereas that of woman is instinctively plural and simultaneous. It is for this reason, Richardson declares, that 'she can move, as it were in all directions at once, why, with a man-astonishing ease, she can "take up" everything by turns, while she "originates" nothing' (405). The inconsistency and contradictions that will characterise Molly Bloom's narrative, are here defined by Richardson not as a mark of women's lack or weakness of intellect and structured thought (this is merely men's interpretation of something they cannot understand), but a demonstration of the ability of the female consciousness to conceive the continuity of things, and to see life 'whole and harmonious' (404).

While Richardson reappropriates the womanly woman for feminism, 're-reading' it in the manner she had advocated in her 1917 essay, she nevertheless refused to channel her own female consciousness into the feminine art of creating social harmony. It is significant that in 'Women and the Future' Richardson cites H. G. Wells as the 'chief spokesman' of what she sees as the common male reading of egoism in women, for it was through her resistance to Wells' self-assertive masculinity that she honed her concept of a specifically female literary aesthetic. '*I* don't want to exercise the feminine art', Miriam Henderson declares to Wells' fictional persona Hypo Wilson in *Revolving Lights*, protesting against his attempt to recruit her as 'a useful fiercely loyal creature', working intelligently but submissively in support of his own writing and theories (*P* III: 258, 253). The heated debate that takes place between them, one of the set-pieces in *Pilgrimage* in which Richardson sets forth her thinking on women and aesthetics, presents many of the key ideas that the 'Woman and the Future' essay would repeat almost verbatim the following year. Miriam tries to explain to Wilson, for example, that women have long been pre-eminent in the 'art of making atmospheres', although '[n]ot one man in a million is aware of it' (257), and elaborates Richardson's idea of female egoism and women's synthetic consciousness: 'Views and opinions are masculine things. Women are indifferent to them really. . . . women can hold all opinions at once, or any, or none. It's because they see the relations of things which don't change, more than things which are always changing, and mostly the importance to men of the things they believe. But behind it all their own lives are untouched' (259).

Miriam is determined to embrace that untouched life rather than to hide it, just as Richardson was determined that her own feminine art would truthfully express women's 'completely self-centered consciousness'. To do so, however, it needed to break free from the fetters of masculine theories, values and linguistic and narrative conventions, which Richardson thought incompatible with the quality of female consciousness she wanted to convey, and this was not easy. In *The Tunnel* Miriam thinks that a truly female voice could never be understood by men: '[i]n speech with a man a woman is at a disadvantage – because they speak

THE WOMANLY WOMAN

Where Molly Bloom and Miriam Henderson do bear similarity is in their egoism, associated with feminine narcissism and indifference in Molly but reappropriated by Richardson as a key characteristic of female self-identity that is entirely impossible for the male mind to understand. Richardson's conception of woman as 'the essential egoist' is elaborated in her theory of the 'womanly woman', in her essay 'Woman and the Future' (1924). Like Woolf's later discussion of the Angel of the House, she was here taking up a popular term for the familiar cultural ideal of femininity. Unlike Woolf, however, she does not reject this concept as a false cultural stereotype, instead transforming the womanly woman from an icon of feminine selflessness into the epitome of female egoism:

> the womanly woman lives, all her life in the deep current of eternity, an individual, self-centered. Because she is one with life, past, present, and future are together in her, unbroken. Because she thinks flowingly, with her feelings, she is relatively indifferent to the fashions of men, to the momentary arts, religions, philosophies, and sciences, valuing them only in so far as she is aware of their importance in the evolution of the beloved. It is man's incomplete individuality that leaves him at the mercy of that subtle form of despair which is called ambition, and accounts for his apparent selfishness. Only completely self-centered consciousness can attain to unselfishness – the celebrated unselfishness of the womanly woman. Only a complete self, carrying all its goods in its own hands, can go out, perfectly, to others, to move freely in any direction. Only a complete self can afford to man the amusing spectacle of the chameleon woman. (Kime Scott, 1990: 413)

Female egoism, Richardson asserts, is not to be confused simply with 'masculine selfishness', for it has far more 'depth and scope'. It is by keeping faith with the egoism of essential womanhood that the 'womanly woman' can be truly unselfish, for it is exactly because of this intuitive faith in herself (an awareness of her Bergsonian 'duration') that she does not need to proclaim her identity in the external manner of men. Being complete in herself, moreover, and therefore indifferent to all external theories and beliefs, is what allows 'her gift of imaginative sympathy, her capacity for vicarious living' (414), her ability to take up one or other idea if it is important to those around her. The womanly woman may seem, to male eyes, a supportive and submissive 'angel of the house', but it is a role that she takes on deliberately out of love and responsibility, and in full knowledge of her superior synthetic consciousness. This, Richardson proclaims, is the long-standing 'genius' of women, constituting a form of social (although consciously self-denying) art that has gone unrecognised within masculine culture. Virginia Woolf's representation of Mrs Ramsay in *To the Lighthouse*, very much a 'womanly woman' in Richardson's sense, suggests that she too regarded such social art as a creative skill specific to women.

different languages. She may understand his. Hers he will never speak or understand. In pity, or from other motives, she must therefore, stammeringly, speak his. He listens and is flattered and thinks he has her measure when he has not touched even the fringe of her consciousness' (*P* II: 210). It is an idea repeated in *Oberland*, when she argues with the Italian Guerini over the uselessness of 'centuries of masculine attempts to represent women only in relation to the world as known to men':

> It was then he was angry.
> 'How else are they to be represented?'
> 'They can't be represented by men. Because by every word they use men and women mean different things'. (*P* IV: 93)

We return here to the concept of the gendered sentence, and the possibility of a 'feminine' style of writing that might subvert the entrenched structures of masculine thought. Like Woolf, however, Richardson also distinguishes the so-called 'feminine' psychological realism of writers such as James and Joyce from her own expression of female consciousness. This is because she regards even these male writers as being primarily concerned with method over material, with technique and 'ways of doing things', as Wyndham Lewis complained of Joyce, more for their own sake than in the service of the things they represent. It is a debateable argument, but one that is in accordance with her view of men as inherently concerned with 'doing' rather than 'being'. While Miriam Henderson is at first fascinated and enthralled by the impressionist style of James' *The Ambassadors*, she later complains to Wilson of the 'self-satisfied, complacent, know-all condescendingness' of his method (*P* IV: 239). Miriam is thinking of James and Jospeh Conrad in this passage, but Richardson writing in 1931 might also have had Joyce in mind, both being writers whose psychological method she admired, but whose blatant delight in their own skill was for Richardson typically 'male'. One of the main characteristics of 'men's books', according to Miriam Henderson, is that they are 'unable to make you forget them, the authors, for a moment' (*P* IV: 239). When Richardson reviewed *Finnegans Wake* in 1939, she noted the skill of Joyce's 'long, lyrically wailing, feminine monologue' but picked out for emphasis the passage quoted above in which he drew attention to the ultimate control of his 'masculine fist' (Kime Scott, 1990: 428). However 'feminine' Joyce's prose might be in style and form, for Richardson it could never do more than approximate female consciousness because it would always remain 'a signed self-portrait', bearing 'its author's [male] signature not only across each sentence, but upon almost every word' (426).

LITERARY ANDROGYNY

Woolf's concept of literary androgyny is put forward in the last chapter of *A Room of One's Own*, and in her typically mock self-effacing style is presented as something of an afterthought, prompted by the sight of a young man and woman getting into a taxi together. Struck by the sense of unity that this scene evokes in her, she contemplates the possibility that the human soul is actually made up of both male and female traits, and that although one typically dominates the other within the brain, '[t]he normal and comfortable state of being is when the two live in harmony together, spiritually cooperating' (*AROO*: 128). This, she thinks, might have been what Samuel Taylor Coleridge meant when he declared that 'a great mind is androgynous': 'It is when this fusion takes place that the mind is fully fertilised and uses all its faculties. Perhaps a mind that is purely masculine cannot create, any more than a mind that is purely feminine' (128).

Woolf's concept of the androgynous literary mind, while it is celebrated as an imaginative resistance of social and linguistic gender oppositions by some feminist critics (Heilbrun, 1973; Moi, 1985), has troubled others who construe it as a strategy for evading her social and historical identity and experience as a real woman, escaping instead into the detachment of an impersonal aestheticism (Showalter, 1977; Stubbs 1979). For these readers, her statement that '[i]t is fatal for a woman to lay the least stress on any grievance; to plead even with justice any cause; in any way to speak consciously as a woman' (*AROO*: 136) is a refusal of

ANDROGYNY

Androgyny means ambiguous or neutral sexual identity, although it is often collapsed with the concept of 'hermaphroditism', which refers to the mix of both male and female sexual characteristics. While it is possible to be 'androgynous' in appearance, psychological traits or behaviour, however, 'hermaphrodite' (or more contemporary 'intersexual') is usually applied to the hybrid physiological condition of possessing both male and female physical characteristics or sexual organs. For the Romantic imagination, androgyny signified a transcendence of the physical self and the union of the rational and creative aspects of the mind in the spiritual experience of the sublime. For the late nineteenth century, however, it became a vehicle for the projection of cultural anxieties about the destabilisation of gender, class and ethnic divisions, and an image of ideal, desexualised ethereality to be contrasted with the threatening, monstrous bodily sexuality of the hermaphrodite. As the reference to Coleridge indicates, in *A Room of One's Own* Woolf is thinking of androgyny as a psychic state in the Romantic sense; the reconciliation or balance of two opposing forces within the mind, and a form of creative vision that can move beyond the impediments on artistic expression imposed by the social and material world. This would seem to be a total u-turn on her argument up to this point, and in most of her other critical writing, that the mind of a writer is profoundly influenced by the spirit of his or her age. Moreover, it also means that she does not consider the possibility that Coleridge's advocacy of creative androgyny at once conceals and manifests his own anxieties about 'masculine' and 'feminine' art, and the increasing prominence of women writers and intellectuals within the Romantic period itself. On androgyny and the creative imagination see Heilbrun, 1973; Bazin, 1973; Stevenson, 1996.

solidarity with the very tradition of women's writing that she claims to promote. Yet it is important to recognise the manner of Woolf's thinking in this last chapter, in which she is posing a hypothesis and working through its implications rather than articulating a theory fully formed in advance, as well as her nuanced definition of what it is to write *as* a woman. As part of her fundamental belief in the impartiality of the novelist's perspective, Woolf argued that writers should avoid intentionally thinking of their sex when they wrote; in other words they should not allow either the masculine or feminine side of the mind to overwhelm the other. Yet this is not to say that their writing will not *reveal* their sex, indeed far from it. For Woolf, it is exactly when a woman writer is not preoccupied with fulfilling or resisting the expectations of gender, and thus writes in a way that is culturally androgynous, keeping perfect faith with her artistic 'integrity', that she writes most naturally her own female prose.

In the same year when she gave the two talks at Cambridge that would become *A Room of One's Own*, Woolf published her sixth novel, *Orlando* (1928), a fantastical biography of a time-travelling, sex-changing noble wo/man. Providing a fictional parallel to the theories put forward in the essay, it follows her account of the historical circumstances of the woman writer from the age of Shakespeare to the present, *at the same time* as dramatising the concept of androgyny. Physiologically Orlando is a sequential hermaphrodite, changing from one sex to another rather than possessing both male and female organs at the same time. In all but physical sex, however, he/she is androgynous:

> Orlando had become a woman – there is no denying it. But in every other respect, Orlando remained precisely as he had been. The change of sex, though it altered their future, did nothing whatever to alter their identity. . . . His memory – but in future we must, for convention's sake, say 'her' for 'his', and 'she' for 'he' – her memory then, went back through all the events of her past life without encountering any obstacle. (O: 133)

Orlando's mutation from one sex to another is of course a literal embodiment of the suggestion in *A Room of One's Own* that the human essence contains both male and female elements, one of which usually predominates. More significantly, however, this is paralleled in Orlando's mental state, which vacillates constantly between the two after her transformation. What Woolf also illustrates, however, is her argument that our lives as men and women are conditioned by social and historical circumstance. As Orlando moves from the Elizabethan court, to Stuart London, to the role of English ambassador to Constantinople, he acquires along the way a knowledge of literary tradition, the wealth and status of a dukedom, and the experience of continental travel. As she lives through the later eighteenth, nineteenth and twentieth centuries as a woman, however, Orlando's movements are restricted (her property is taken under the jurisdiction of the law, long skirts hamper her stride and it is her husband Shelmardine who becomes the international traveller, while Orlando waits for him at home). Her pen is similarly constrained (she hides her manuscript when interrupted, is more modest about her literary efforts and dependent on the newly eminent Nick Greene for publication), as a result of the 'Spirit of the Age' and the cultural restrictions of her femininity. Out of a combination of the education, money and contacts inherited from her earlier male self, however, and the social freedom provided by the existence of a supportive but usefully absent husband, Orlando is finally able to fulfil her literary ambitions and become a writer. The poem that earns a prize in the 'Present Day' owes its existence to the full passage of Orlando's male and female history.

SUMMARY

Women's marginality within the history of cultural discourse, and the creation of a literary form and language specifically suited to the expression of female consciousness were significant concerns within Woolf and Richardson's literary feminism. In their critical and fictional writings both were engaged in resisting the patriarchal tradition that pervaded the very structures of social thought and linguistic form, and posed significant practical, ideological and aesthetic obstacles to the prospective woman writer. Where they diverge is that Richardson's literary aesthetic resulted from her belief in the essential difference of the male and female mind, while Woolf's was based in a refusal of that difference, the assertion that gender categories are historically and materially constituted, and an effort to transcend cultural stereotypes of sex and gender by imagining the artistic mind to be 'androgynous', or a mixture of both masculine and feminine qualities. What we have, until this chapter, been reading as Woolf and Richardson's *modernist* experimentation with the novel genre can now be seen as fundamentally linked to their *feminist* determination to portray female consciousness faithfully. Pre-empting more recent feminist critics who have interpreted the formal innovations of the modernist novel as *in themselves* a subversive critique of the social and political status quo, however, both yet also distinguish between the qualities that make their fiction 'modern' and those that make it 'female', or written by a woman. A novel might be modern in form, but only its subject-matter and context can make it female. Woolf and Richardson's distinction between what we might describe as 'formally feminine' and 'politically female' prose was in part honed against the regular association of their literary style with that of Joyce and Marcel Proust. Joyce's depiction of Molly Bloom's consciousness in the final chapter of *Ulysses*, for example, while written in highly experimental interior monologue form, maintains masculine constructions of female identity, however, in order to critique rather than endorse, and indeed all the more insidiously because it assumes an ostensibly female voice in which to do so. Although postmodernist literary feminism has reappropriated Joyce exactly by asserting the political radicalism of his aesthetic experimentalism, the relation of the two cannot be regarded simplistically, as Woolf and Richardson were both aware.

4

TIME AND HISTORY

One of the key characteristics of Joyce, Woolf and Richardson's 'new realism' was their preoccupation with the representation of time. Narrative in the modernist novel typically follows the passage of time as it is experienced within the minds of its characters, rather than the straightforwardly forward-moving plot of standard realism. As a result it might take hundreds of pages to cover the period of only one day, as in Joyce's *Ulysses*, or, as in Woolf's *Orlando*, far less to move across four hundred years. The idea that the experience of time is relative to the individual consciousness was not itself new. What marks the representation of the subjective perception of time at the beginning of the twentieth century, however, is the collective nature of this fascination. The stage had been set from the 1880s, with the standardisation of the Greenwich meridian and the synchronisation of clocks around the world in order to serve the needs of modern transport and communication systems (the railway, the telegraph), the effect of which was to make the passage of time and distance suddenly seem to change in a very obvious and public way. Alongside this regulated *universality* of temporal and spatial measurement, however, both the physical and psychological sciences were paradoxically beginning to reveal its arbitrariness, and the *relativity* of temporal experience (Kern, 1983). The result was a climate of broad debate as people attempted to make sense of the meaning of time and

existence in the modern world. The debacle of the First World War further ruptured any remaining continuity with what seemed by comparison
to be the confident stability of the past, producing a pervasive sense of
historical, social and psychological dislocation.

THE RELATION OF TIME AND SPACE

The idea that time is experienced by the mind as an all-encompassing
flux rather than a linear sequence of events has become one of the
defining principles of the modernist novel, epitomised in Woolf's
description of life in 'Modern Novels' as 'a luminous halo, a semi-trans-
parent envelope surrounding us from the beginning of consciousness to
the end'. We have already seen the problem with any simple interpretation of Woolf's critical review of her fellow 'Georgians' as a manifesto
for her own aesthetic aims. Neither should we assume, moreover, that
her description of the relation of time and the mind was particularly
original; indeed for the majority of her contemporary readers, her
argument would have been contextualised within current and topical
theories and debate about the perception and relations of time and
space.

The writer perhaps most widely credited with responding to Bergson's
theories is the French novelist Marcel Proust (the two were related by
marriage), whose À la recherche du temps perdu (In Search of Lost Time,
1913–27) is a long study of the mental experience of time. Yet Proust's
fiction is more of an examination of time in the mind than its direct
expression. Richardson recognised this, and while admiring his writing,
nevertheless noted: 'He is not, as has been said, writing *through* consciousness, but *about* consciousness, a vastly different enterprise' (*LDR*:
64; my italics). What she draws attention to here is the difference
between their literary aims and methods; Proust's novel being a *reflection
upon* the subjective experience of time and memory, very different from
her own attempt to capture perceptual conscious experience *as it occurs*
within the strict prism of Miriam's attention and understanding at any
one time. Bergson himself made a similar distinction when discussing
the ways in which a novelist might represent a character's psychic state at
a given moment:

DURATION

One of the key examples with which Henri Bergson illustrated his theory of the fundamental incompatibility between the intuitive and rational self was the experience of time. Time as it is lived freely by the consciousness, he argues, is very different from time as we have come to understand it through the authoritative yet arbitrary configurations of the clock and the calendar. It is through the subjective consciousness that we experience time as it really is, a continuum in which past and present interpenetrate or melt into each other. Bergson calls this *la durée* or 'duration'. The rational mind, however, can only comprehend time by organising it into a linear and advancing sequence of standardised, measurable units, *spatialising* the 'real' time of duration into 'clock-time'. For Bergson duration and clock-time are not separate phenomena; time *only* exists as duration, and the clock is merely the convenient but inadequate means by which a mechanistic world conceives and represents it. Bergson's theory of duration is inextricably linked to his concept of memory. In *Matter and Memory* (1896; 1911), mirroring the distinction he makes between clock-time and real time, he argues that there are two kinds of memory: 'habit' memory, in which the mind consciously repeats to itself the scene of a previous event or experience, and 'pure' memory or 'contemplation', which is unconscious, imageless and only revealed in dreams or moments of intuition. The first is automatic and breaks up memory into separate observable instances, the second instinctive and spontaneous, in which memory is continuous (Bergson, 1911). Duration involves the experience of continuous pure memory from an awareness of the present moment. In prioritising time over space (unconscious, imageless, continuous duration over consciously externalised, separate and therefore observable matter), Bergson's philosophy redefines our understanding of existence, which in his theories becomes predicated on creative intuition rather than empirical or scientific observation.

the deeper psychic states . . . express and sum up the whole of our past history: if Paul knows all the conditions under which Peter acts, we must suppose that no detail of Peter's life escapes him, and that his imagination reconstructs and even lives over again Peter's history. But we must here make a vital distinction. When *I myself pass through* a certain psychic state, I know exactly the intensity of this state and its importance in relation to the others, not by measurement or comparison, but because the intensity of e.g. a deep-seated feeling is nothing else than the feeling itself. On the other hand, if I try to give you an *account* of this psychic state, I shall be unable to make you realize its intensity except by some definite sign of a mathematical kind. (Bergson, 2001: 185)

If Paul is to experience the real intensity of Peter's experience, Bergson notes, he must *become* Peter, just as Richardson, in writing through Miriam's consciousness rather than giving an account of it, *becomes* Miriam. While denying that Bergson's theories had any direct impact on her writing, Richardson admitted that he 'influenced many minds, if only by putting into words something then dawning within the human consciousness' (Kumar, 1959: 495). Certainly in *Pilgrimage* she closely approximates his challenge to the modern novelist to capture the fundamental human self in the ever-present quality of its 'perpetual state of becoming' (Bergson, 2001: 130).

Bergson claimed that his theories about the experience and relation of time and space in the mind anticipated the work in the physical sciences of Albert Einstein, specifically his concept of relativity, an attack on the belief that man can have absolute knowledge of physical time or space. Einstein's theories of special and general relativity demonstrated that time and space needed to be understood as inseparable: as a combination of three-dimensional space *plus* a fourth dimension of time which he argued together constituted the physical history of the universe. As Einstein's former tutor Herman Minkowski (1864–1909) described it in a paper on the recent experiments in physics in 1908, '[h]enceforth space by itself, and time by itself, are doomed to fade away into mere shadows, and only a kind of union of the two will preserve an independent reality' (Lorentz *et al.*, 1952: 75).

Both Bergson and Einstein were celebrity figures in the 1910s and 1920s, whose lecture tours were attended by a wide public. The success of the solar eclipse expedition, which was widely covered in the popular press, along with a flood of abridged accounts of the principle of relativity, indeed meant that even an awareness of terms such as 'atoms' and 'electromagnetic waves' quickly permeated beyond scientific circles.

The concepts and terminology of subjective and scientific relativity become prominent in Joyce, Woolf and Richardson's non-fictional and fictional writings in the 1920s and 1930s. Joyce mentions both Bergson and Einstein in *Finnegans Wake*. Woolf, as noted earlier, knew of Bergson through her Bloomsbury companions, and the comment in *Orlando* about the 'extraordinary discrepancy between time on the clock and time in the mind' clearly paraphrases the key terms of his philosophy. Bloomsbury also provided an arena for the dissemination of scientific ideas (Bertrand Russell published two popularisations, *The ABC of Atoms* in 1923 and *The*

ALBERT EINSTEIN (1879–1955) AND THE THEORY OF RELATIVITY

Albert Einstein was a German physicist whose groundbreaking theories of 'special' (1905) and 'general' (1916) relativity transformed previous scientific understanding of the relations of time and space. In the first he demonstrated that time does not pass at a fixed rate because the experience of time is relative to the degree of motion of the observer (depending on the position of the observer, distances either seem to compress or stretch, and clocks to run faster or more slowly). Measurements of time cannot therefore have absolute, universal meaning. In the second he expanded the concept of relativity to take in the effect of gravity, showing that space bends in relation to matter. Relativity is difficult to understand because it only becomes apparent when very high speeds or vast distances are being considered. Thus to the normal eye it seems counterintuitive. Einstein's hypotheses were proved by the British eclipse expedition to South Africa in 1919, led by Arthur Eddington, professor of astrophysics at Cambridge, which demonstrated that starlight was bent by the mass of the sun. Note that the theory of relativity is *not* the same as relativ*ism* – the principle that moral and epistemological theories are not absolute but dependent on context and point of view, and that all beliefs are therefore equally valid – and does not imply that nothing can be 'known'. Einstein described it perhaps more accurately but less famously as a theory of 'invariances', which refers to the principle that objective facts in relation to specific conditions can be observed. Relativity applies to the wider frame of spacetime but does not deny knowledge within social relations and the human realm. For a layman-friendly introduction to Einstein's relativity see Kennedy, 2003. For the popular reception of his work in the 1920s see Friedman and Donley, 1985; Whitworth, 2002.

ABC of Relativity in 1925), and although Woolf admitted to finding Einstein difficult she did read the physicist and mathematician James Jeans' best-selling *The Mysterious Universe* (1930). Dorothy Richardson wrote in a letter in 1946 that while she thought that 'all metaphors, as ever, like all language & all art & all science, are inadequate to convey reality', nevertheless 'if Einstein is on the right track, a centre, unfathomable, would seem to come nearest' (*LDR*: 549).

The idea that scientific laws themselves are universalised conventions, and that the empirical observation of time and place will always be contingent on the position of the observer, of course provided additional support to the aesthetic and social rejection of the novelistic conventions of authorial omniscience, narrative chronology and situated plot. As many early readers noted, both Joyce in *Ulysses* and Woolf in *Mrs Dalloway* employ a montage technique comparable with that of film in order to depict snapshots of life as it coexists across the city of Dublin or London. The 'Wandering Rocks' section of the former, for example, seems a tour de force of spatial and temporal simultaneity, in which characters and events from across the wider novel intercalate in nineteen scenes, linked by the journeys through the city of Father Conmee and the British viceroy. A similar strategy is employed by Woolf, as the thoughts of people going about their separate errands are briefly concentrated and drawn together by an aeroplane drawing an advertisement in the sky, or the stately car bearing the crest of government. It is this that gives both novels their 'cinematic' effect of presenting different events taking place in different places at once. Within the context of Einstein's physics, however, the idea that simultaneity can be observed in this way, or in other words that measurements of space and time are fixed and universal and therefore comparable, was refuted. That an event in one location happens at the same time as another event in a different location, Einstein argued in his 1905 paper on special relativity, is impossible to deduce without a standard frame of reference from which to make the comparison. Whatever frame of reference forms that standard, however, can only be arbitrary, because it is just one out of any number of possibilities; what seems simultaneous to one observer will not seem so to another.

Mrs Dalloway, like *Ulysses*, is formally structured by the motif of the passing hours of the day, set in this case by the standard of Big Ben.

Again like Joyce's novel, however, it undercuts that structure, both mentally (emphasising the inability of an hour on the clock to mark the experience of 'duration' in the mind), and scientifically (exposing the arbitrariness of the standardisation of time). Big Ben is not the only clock in *Mrs Dalloway*, however much it may be granted the superiority of dictating the time of the day. Just after it finishes booming half-past eleven, for example, Peter Walsh hears the clock of St Margaret's, following slightly in the wake of her authoritative masculine counterpart: 'I am not late. No, it is precisely half-past eleven, she says. Yet, though she is perfectly right, her voice, being the voice of the hostess, is reluctant to inflict its individuality' (*MD*: 64). Thirty minutes later, when Clarissa lays out a dress on her bed as Rezia and Septimus Smith walk along Harley Street, the reader is told '[I]t was precisely twelve o'clock; twelve by Big Ben' (*MD*: 122). Scientific relativity here serves to parallel Woolf's critique of the cultural norms of society (represented by the figure of Sir William Bradshaw, medical consultant and custodian of the principle of 'divine proportion'), determined to deny and confine all that challenges and disrupts its dominant, rational (and masculine) order.

'SPACETIME'

If relativity's challenge to epistemology, or the ways in which we can be said to 'know', contributed to the formal experimentation with narrative and chronology in the modernist novel, it also posed ontological questions about the ultimate nature of existence and being that coalesce with its redefinition of subject identity, memory and history. One of the most direct references to the modern challenge to conventional authoritative theories of existence is the 'Ithaca' section of *Ulysses*, which Joyce described as 'a mathematico-astronomico-physico-mechanico-geometrico-chemico sublimation of Bloom and Stephen' (*LJJ*: 161). To Frank Budgen he explained:

> I am writing *Ithaca* in the form of a mathematical catechism. All events are resolved into their cosmic physical, psychical &c equivalents . . . so that not only will the reader know everything and know it in the baldest coldest way, but

> Bloom and Stephen therefore become heavenly bodies, wanderers like the
> stars at which they gaze. (*LJJ* I: 159–60)

The penultimate episode of *Ulysses*, the close of the Stephen/Bloom
part of the novel, and a review of the events of the day, 'Ithaca' parodies
and debates various parallel yet mutually inconsistent and ultimately
unsatisfactory theories for explaining man's existence and his relation to
the universe. Because the novel is set in 1904 there can be no conscious
reference to Einstein in either of their thoughts, although Bloom, for
example, has knowledge of antecedent theories and discoveries in
astronomy, evolution and physical mathematics. Joyce, however, having
by now left the interior monologue style of the early episodes long
behind, is not restricted to the limits of internal perspective, and through
the question-and-answer format of the catechism is able both to put over
Stephen's and Bloom's divergent beliefs and opinions, and to question
and critique the grounds for those beliefs through the coldly detached
voice of the narrator/questioner. The narrative thus moves constantly
between a microcosmic focus on Stephen and Bloom themselves as they
walk to Eccles Street and drink cocoa in the kitchen, to the macrocosmic
theories of science, within which they are lost amidst the infinity of the
universe.

Man's utter inconsequence within the larger scheme of physical science is brutally demonstrated in the long passage in which Bloom
expounds recent astronomical, evolutionary, geological and cosmological
theories as he points out astronomical constellations in the night sky to
the departing Stephen. From the arrangement of the stars he moves on
to:

> Meditations of evolution increasingly vaster: of the infinite lattiginous scintillating
> uncondensed milky way, discernible by daylight by an observer placed at the
> lower end of a cylindrical vertical shaft 5000 ft deep sunk from the surface
> towards the centre of the earth: of Sirius (alpha in Canis Maior) 10 lightyears
> (57,000,000,000,000 miles) distant and in volume 900 times the dimension of
> our planet: . . . of our system plunging towards the constellation of Hercules: of
> the parallax or parallactic drift of socalled fixed stars, in reality evermoving wan-
> derers from immeasurably remote eons to infinitely remote futures in compar-

ison with which the years, threescore and ten, of allotted human life formed a
parenthesis of infinitesimal brevity. (*U*: 819)

And from the infinite spatio-temporal enormity of the universe to the
relatively finite yet equally incomprehensible history of the planet and its
species:

Of the eons of geological periods recorded in the stratifications of the earth: of
the myriad minute entomological organic existences concealed in cavities of the
earth, beneath removable stones, in hives and mounds, of microbes, germs,
bacteria, bacilli, spermatozoa: of the incalculable trillions of billions of millions of
imperceptible molecules contained by cohesion of molecular affinity in a single
pinhead: of the universe of human serum constellated with red and white
bodies, themselves universes of void space constellated with other bodies,
each, in continuity, its universe of divisible component bodies of which each
was again divisible in divisions of redivisible component bodies, dividends and
divisors ever diminishing without actual division till, if the progress were carried
far enough, nought nowhere was never reached. (819–20)

The very exhaustiveness of such classificatory systems of existence, which
when compared both imply and refuse parallel and pattern, makes them
seemingly meaningless; as, the reader suspects, Joyce also implies. But
perhaps most significantly they are incapable of answering the one large
question that lies behind the episode's catechetical style: what is the
origin of existence? Despite there surely being one, however far back in
time man goes, however microscopic in space he looks, the process of
division seems to continue into the nothingness of infinity. The 'logical
conclusion' (823) that is drawn from Bloom's rendering of their different
accounts is described in terms that suggest the finite infinity of Einstein's
gravitational universe, the notion of

an infinity renderable equally finite by the suppositious apposition of one or more
bodies equally of the same and of different magnitudes: a mobility of illusory
forms immobilised in space, remobilised in air: a past which possibly had
ceased to exist as a present before its probable spectators had entered actual
present existence. (823).

While many non-physicists mistakenly identify relativity and relativism, Joyce delighted in the parodical possibilities of their deceptive likeness, and it is perhaps thus not surprising that the demonstration of theories of existence in 'Ithaca' as *relative* ends in an assertion of *relativity*. Significantly, moreover, Joyce's relativity does not deny human meaning. When Stephen defines himself, for example, with typical abstract intellectualism, as 'a conscious rational animal proceeding syllogistically from the known to the unknown . . . between a micro and a macrocosm ineluctably constructed upon the incertitude of the void', his assertion is countered by Bloom's here-and-now pride (having left his key behind he has had to climb over the railings and let himself in through the service door) that 'as a competent keyless citizen he had proceeded energetically *from the unknown to the known* through the incertitude of the void' (818; my italics). In Bloom's down-to-earth resistance against the meaninglessness of existence in the big scheme of things, and his assertion that within the contracted frame of social life he has managed to get himself to the quite literally 'known' space of his kitchen, Joyce articulates the everyday reality of man's practical relation to the infinite complexity of his world. Bloom the modern Odysseus has finally reached home, but as he lies in bed with Molly both are nevertheless still part of a wider, continuous movement: 'At rest relatively to themselves and to each other. In motion being each and both carried westward, forward and rereward respectively, by the proper perpetual motion of the earth through everchanging tracks of neverchanging space' (870).

While the relativity of spacetime means that simultaneity is impossible to observe, over very long distances it has the opposite effect of making events that take place days or years apart seem to happen at once; the light given out by even the closest star, for example, will have taken years to reach the point where it is observed from earth in the present. For Richardson the multi-dimensional infinitude of spacetime provided a model for the expanse of the individual consciousness. '[I]s it not odd', she wrote on the possibilities of Einsteinian metaphor,

> considering yourself an infinitesimal speck upon speck travelling through space, that you are nevertheless able to go ahead & ahead, to travel, more swiftly than light, through no matter what vast distances; that the 'cosmos', no matter how

extensive, is too small to imprison your consciousness, & that however far things go, you can outstrip them & reach a region, maybe a centre . . . whence comes, or flows, or streams, or radiates, whatever-you-like-to-call-it, that keeps things going. (*LDR*: 549)

Woolf explores a similar idea in *Orlando*, using the fantasy of physical time-travel in order to write the spacetime biography of her hero/ine over a period of four hundred years. For Woolf scientific theory suggests the expanse of not only individual consciousness but also a continuous, historical consciousness that extends from our ancestors into the present. At the same time, however, she refuses to advocate entirely transcending the significance of time as it is lived socially within common, everyday experience. Consider the following passage, in which Orlando speeds through time into the present moment:

The immensely long tunnel in which she seemed to have been travelling for hundreds of years widened; the light poured in; her thoughts became mysteriously tightened . . . she could hear every whisper and crackle in the room so that the clock ticking on the mantelpiece beat like a hammer. And so for some seconds the light went on becoming brighter and brighter, and she saw everything more and more clearly and the cloud ticked louder and louder until there was a terrific explosion right in her ear. Orlando leapt as if she had been violently struck on the head. Ten times she was struck. In fact it was ten o'clock in the morning. It was the eleventh of October. It was 1928. It was the present moment. (*O*: 284)

At first Orlando is surrounded by darkness, because in order to cross time she must be moving faster than light. It is only as she reaches her destination that light catches up and begins to surround her. Once she is still relative to the world around her, the clock and the calendar reassert themselves, reminding her of their social hegemony as they do throughout the novel whenever the narrator or Orlando herself most challenge the limits of conventional time.

Woolf the creative artist may be fascinated with metaphors of cosmological relativity, but Woolf the material historian remembers that to the ordinary eye the experience of space and time will remain to all intents and purposes static and absolute. What preoccupies her thinking on reality and its representation throughout her writing was how to balance these conflicting aspects of reality. 'Now is life very solid or very shifting?' she asked in her diary in January 1929, two months after the publication of *Orlando*:

> I am haunted by the two contradictions. This has gone on for ever: will last for ever; goes down to the bottom of the world, this moment I stand on. Also it is transitory, flying, diaphanous . . . Perhaps it may be that though we change; one flying after another, so quick, so quick, yet we are somehow successive, & continuous – we human beings; & show the light through. But what is the light? (*D* III: 218)

Light, which Einstein's physics had proved to be the one thing that is constant and universal within spacetime, was central to the planning of Woolf's new novel, *The Moths*. Evoking the image of diaphanous insects drawn in currents to light, the title was only changed to *The Waves* when she discovered that moths are nocturnal and do not fly in the day, the alternative possibly suggested by the fact that light was a form of electromagnetic wave, and its importance within the new physics.

Throughout the evolution of the novel, scientific and spiritual metaphors are shared. Woolf was already conceiving a 'very serious, mystical poetical work' in her diary in March 1927, in which she would present 'time all telescoped into one lucid channel' (131), an image that suggests both the time-travelling scene of *Orlando* and the scientific phenomenon of light rays. In June 1927 she and Leonard had joined the crowds of people who travelled to North Yorkshire to watch the first total eclipse of the sun for over two hundred years. She described the experience afterwards as one of spiritual extinction: 'We had seen the world dead. This was within the power of nature' (*D* III: 144). At the moment of the eclipse of light the rhythm of the waves (both the electro-magnetic waves of light, and for Woolf the continuous rhythm of inner life or Bergsonian memory) seems to stop. Her account of the sudden darkness, the wraith-like feeling of the watchers, and the colour and otherworldly beauty of the refracted light that followed, is repeated with similar emphasis by Bernard: 'How then does light return to the world after the eclipse of the sun?', he asks, 'how describe the world seen without a self?' (*W*: 238, 239).

In 1928 the novel is again envisaged as 'an abstract mystical eyeless book' (*D* III: 203). In May 1929 Woolf declares, 'I am not trying to tell a story . . . I shall do away with exact place & time' (229, 230). She imagines beginning with various independent characters, surrounding them with the 'unreal word', 'the phantom waves' (236). By October she was observing, 'never, in my life, did I attack such a vague yet elaborate design; whenever I make a mark I have to think of its relation to a dozen others' (259), and in November writing of her concern to provide some solid human standard to set against the continuous movement of the waves: 'I am convinced that I am right to seek for a station whence I can set my people against time & the sea – but Lord, the difficulty of digging oneself in there, with conviction' (264). One such 'station' is the figure of Percival, who as the representative of a previous positivist paradigm of existence, provides a reference point for the subjective soliloquies of the six other characters and their relative perceptions of the world. As they wait for him in a restaurant, for example, Neville thinks that 'without Percival there is no solidity. We are silhouettes, hollow phantoms moving mistily without a background' (*W*: 100). When he arrives they are immediately organised into a united whole, their differences endowed with underlying connections. Frequently described in relation to the sun, they form themselves, like the solar system, in relation to his mass, and after his death have to readjust. 'The lights of the world have gone out', Neville despairs, and, recalling Woof's description of the aftermath of the eclipse, 'Oh, to crumple this telegram in my fingers – to let the light of the world flood back' (124). 'About him my feeling was', Bernard observes, 'he sat there in the centre. Now I go that spot no longer. The place is empty' (126).

At the end of 1930, when Woolf was finishing the novel, she records a discussion with Lytton Strachey and her brother-in-law Clive Bell about Jeans' recently published *The Mysterious Universe*. 'Talk about the riddle of the universe (Jeans' book) whether it will be known', she notes, adding significantly, 'found out suddenly: about rhythm in prose' (*D* III: 337). Four days later, while writing Bernard's final soliloquy, she reflects, 'the theme effort, effort, dominates: not the waves: & personality: & defiance: but I am not sure of the effect artistically; because the proportions may need the intervention of the waves finally so as to make a conclusion'

(339). Here, as in *Ulysses*, the elaborate relations of the 'unreal' universe and its 'phantom' waves are defied in a prioritising of human character. Cast into doubt about 'the fixity of tables, the reality of here and now', Bernard the artist yet ultimately refuses the explanations of science as being enough to explain reality as it is lived, 'taking upon [himself] the mystery of things' (*W*: 243). Like Leopold Bloom, in the face of the abstract universe he reasserts the reality of everyday life: 'I shaved and washed; did not wake my wife, and had breakfast; put on my hat, and went out to earn my living. After Monday, Tuesday comes' (223). It is the very role of the writer, he proclaims, to tell the story of a human life, for 'if there are no stories, what end can there be, or what beginning?' (223). What this constitutes is yet something like a spacetime of the infinite relations and possibilities of the human consciousness, or the conscious articulation of Bergson's duration and pure memory. 'Thus when I come to shape here at this table between my hands the story of my life and set it before you as a complete thing,' he declares, 'I have to recall things gone far, gone deep, sunk into this life or that and become part of it; dreams, too, things surrounding me . . . shadows of people one might have been; unborn selves' (241).

PREHISTORY AND CULTURAL MEMORY

The trajectory of the modernist novel is framed by the two world wars that devastated the first half of the twentieth century: from 1919 when *Ulysses* began to serialise in the *Little Review*, Woolf wrote 'Modern Novels' and Richardson produced her arguably most technically experimental books *The Tunnel* and *Interim*, to 1938/9, when Joyce's 'Work in Progress' finally appeared as *Finnegans Wake*, Woolf set *Between the Acts* (1941) and *Pilgrimage* was published in collected form. While its first decade was dominated by the cultural and psychological trauma of the First World War and its impact on the processes of memory and representation (Hynes, 1990; Tate, 1998; Sherry, 2003), its second, darkened by the threat of German invasion and another war, turned to the more extended past of national and cultural heritage. In *Ulysses* and *Mrs Dalloway*, as we have seen, contemporary Dublin and London provide 'to the moment' settings for the exploration of the private consciousness and memories of the individual mind.

In *Finnegans Wake* and *Between the Acts* the focus becomes an instinctive, universal human consciousness, and a history of existence particularised through the cultural and literary memory of Ireland and England. Both critique the dominant historical narratives by which national cultural identity is formed and sustained, and the persistent hostility and impulse to oppression that they conceal, exploring (while yet remaining sceptical about) the possibility of art to intervene in, rewrite or subvert them.

Neither Joyce nor Woolf was remotely patriotic in the sense of nationalistic partisanship, and indeed regarded themselves as exiles from the values of their respective countries. Joyce removed himself both physically and linguistically from the domination of British colonialism and the cultural paralysis of Irish nationalism, the idiosyncratic word-play of *Finnegans Wake* continuing the rebellion expressed by the young Stephen Dedalus in *A Portrait of the Artist as a Young Man* against the English language:

> The language in which we are speaking is his before it is mine. . . . His language, so familiar and so foreign, will always be for me an acquired speech. I have not made or accepted its words. My voice holds them at bay. (*PA*: 189)

'I'd like a language which is above all languages, a language to which all will do service', Joyce himself declared, 'I cannot express myself in English without enclosing myself in a tradition' (Ellmann, 1982: 397). Woolf equated English patriotism with patriarchal imperialism and militarism, declaring in *Three Guineas* (1938) that 'as a woman, I have no country. As a woman I want no country. As a woman my country is the whole world' (*AROO*: 313). For both writers the reclaiming of the past from the hegemony of colonialist and patriarchal history was an increasingly important impulse in their fiction.

Begun in the early 1920s and published on the eve of the Second World War, *Finnegans Wake* is written as a night-time dream narrative, through which surfaces the repressed content of a collective human unconscious, and as such is in direct contrast to the conscious and individualised day-time narratives of *Ulysses*. As a result Joyce does away with obviously independent 'characters' in the sense of a Stephen or Bloom, the conscious individual ego replaced instead by a series of narrators (HCE, his wife ALP and their sons Shem and Shaun) who themselves metamorphose. Stylistically, moreover, as with Molly Bloom's monologue, this would require a refusal of linguistic norms and conventions. 'In writing of the night, I really could not, I felt I could not, use words in their ordinary connections', Joyce told the American writer and editor Max Eastman, because '[u]sed that way they do not express how things are in the night, in the different stages – conscious, then semi-conscious, then unconscious' (Ellmann, 1982: 546).

The passage of human existence repeats itself, Joyce asserts in *Finnegans Wake*, as the story of the Earwicker family in Dublin and the proliferation of other parallel myths, legends, historical accounts and anecdotes demonstrates. Despite their specific details, all follow a universal pattern: a fall from original harmony into a constantly repeating battle of hostile opposites. Canonical history, and the canonical fiction that reflects it, does not present objective facts as it purports to do, but a fictional narrative of human progress (typically told by the 'civilised' victors) that represses or silences this universal cycle of conflict and violence beneath the myth of progressive Western development.

In *Finnegans Wake* Joyce allows the chaotic, heterogeneous past, still contained within the unconscious, to subvert the authoritative conventions of history, fiction and language itself. As in *Ulysses* these are mapped onto a division of masculine and feminine essence, in which the first represents an impulse to social, sexual, political and linguistic domination and order and the latter to synthesis and flux. As a 'night-book' *Finnegans Wake* follows the principle of the latter, Joyce forming a critique of canonical Western history out of those very elements that history has discarded as forbidden and unmentionable, and a stylistically complex, dizzying and comic 'reamalgamerge' out of its historical, fictional and philosophical narratives and language. Resisting the kind of conventional narrative written by the domineering Shaun in his 'trifolium librotto, the authordux Book of Lief' (*FW*: 425), the 'story' of *Finnegans Wake* is that attempted by the forger and plagiarist Shem the Penman, a self-portrait of Joyce himself, and eventually told by ALP in her incarnation as the river Liffey, moving from the purity of her origin in the mountains to her polluted, debris-laden extinction as she flows out into the sea, to begin the cycle of both her existence and that of the novel again. *Finnegans Wake* is not unreadable, but it demands that its readers relinquish their own

GIAMBATTISTA VICO (1668–1744)

Just as the structure of *Ulysses* was based loosely on Homer's *Odyssey*, *Finnegans Wake* is based (even more loosely) on the Italian philosopher and historian Giambattista Vico's theory of a cyclical, universal history of human nature. Professor of Rhetoric at the University of Naples, Vico suggested that this was revealed in the cultural inheritance of language, ideas and customs passed down through the generations. Within the particular development of all nations and cultures, he argued, it is possible to identify three stages of universal history in the development of civilization out of barbarism: 'divine', 'heroic' and 'human'. The first two stages are relatively primitive and passionate, man interpreting his world through spiritual faith in myths or gods, and then transferring that faith onto imagined heroes. In the 'human' stage, however, as man becomes more civilized, his passion is controlled by the development of reason and reflection. As the human age progresses this reason gradually collapses in a regression to barbaric instincts of greed and corruption. In response new leaders come to the fore, promoting a new simplicity and religious faith that begins the cycle afresh. Vico's most famous work is *Scienza Nuova* (*The New Science*, first published in 1725; substantially revised in 1730 and again in 1744). Joyce was interested in Vico throughout his literary career, Richard Ellmann noting that he had discussed the *Scienza Nuovo* as early as 1911–13 with one of his language pupils in Trieste, Paolo Cuzzi, to whom he said he thought that Vico anticipated some of the ideas of Sigmund Freud (Ellmann, 1982: 340). In 1926, having directed Harriet Weaver to Vico as a source for *Work in Progress*, he wrote to her with characteristic perversity, 'I would not pay overmuch attention to these theories, beyond using them for all they are worth' (*LJJ* I: 241). Ten years later he was still recommending Vico as a context for reading his own work, telling the Danish writer Tom Kristensen, 'my imagination grows when I read Vico as it doesn't when I read Freud or Jung' (Ellmann, 1982: 693). Vico's hypothesis that Homeric poetry was not the work of one man but represents instead the inherited oral culture of the Greek people, and that the figure of Homer the poet as he has been passed down in history thus offers an example of the universal 'mythic' creation of heroes by primitive man, may also have contributed to Joyce's use of the *Odyssey* in *Ulysses*.

faith and dependence on the world of 'wideawake language, cutanddry grammar and goahead prose'. 'Herenow chuck English and learn to pray plain. . . . Think in your stomach', the novel advises.

For Virginia Woolf, writing in the midst of the bleakest period of the Second World War, the positive hope contained in the cyclical character of the *Wake* seemed impossible. 'We pour to the edge of a precipice', she wrote in June 1940, '& then? I cant conceive that there will be a 27th June 1941' (*D* V: 299). Set six weeks before the start of the war, *Between the Acts* is both a critique of the history of the masculine will to power, and at the same time an elegy to the English past in the face of its potential destruction. As in *Finnegans Wake* this takes the form of the parodic subversion of dominant, patriarchal, imperial, canonical history and literature, this time through the amateur acting, cheap costumery and comic solemnity of Miss LaTrobe's pageant, but also the *alternative* narrative of past and present continuity that is created from the interaction of players and audience as they remember and misremember broken fragments of literary quotation and allusion.

During the writing of *Between the Acts* Woolf was reading Sigmund Freud's work on primitive instinct and the herd mentality characteristic of human group behaviour. Profoundly depressed by the determinism of his theories, she noted in her diary that 'Freud is upsetting . . . If we're all instinct, the unconscious, what's all this about civilisation, the whole man, freedom &c' (*D* V: 250).

SIGMUND FREUD (1856–1939)

In *Civilisation and its Discontents* (1930) and *Moses and Monotheism* (1939), Freud posits that anger and aggression are natural, primitive instincts that are impossible to forget but that are typically repressed to lie latent within the unconscious of 'civilised' man. Violent and destructive acts, whether by an individual or a group, are the result of a breakdown of the restraints of civilisation and the surfacing of this primal desire to destroy and be destroyed. The historical construction of cultural identity, Freud argued, as Joyce does in *Finnegans Wake*, consists in the internalisation of the stories and illusions by which a nation or race sanitises, retells and justifies its past, and the acceptance of such myths as given. *Moses and Monotheism* was received with great controversy because Freud elaborated his theory through the suggestion that Moses had been an Egyptian murdered by the Jews, and that the Christian faith constructed Jesus as a sacrificial redeemer out of guilt for this previous crime.

In *Three Guineas* Woolf takes implicit issue with Freud, arguing that *man*kind's primitive instinct to destruction is exactly that, the natural instinct of men, and that the narratives of patriotism by which it is justified express the voice of only one half, albeit dominant, of human beings. Continuing the theme of *A Room of One's Own*, she suggests that women's long exclusion from positions of power and authority within society means that they have not been either the perpetrators of violence and domination or the authors of history in the way that men have. 'Scarcely a human being in the course of history has fallen to a woman's rifle', she asserts, 'the vast majority of birds and beasts have been killed by you, not by us' (*AROO*: 158). This suggests the possibility that there *is* a way out of a continuously destructive history, and that it lies in the essential difference of female instinct and, even more importantly for Woolf, the alternative social and material history of women's domestic tradition:

> It would seem to follow then as an indisputable fact that 'we' – meaning by 'we' a whole made up of body, brain and spirit, influenced by memory and tradition – must still differ in some essential respects from 'you', whose body, brain and spirit have been so differently trained and are so differently influenced by memory and tradition. Though we see the same world, we see it through different eyes. (175)

Among the villagers watching the pageant in *Between the Acts* the masculine, militarist version of English history is largely internalised by women, who go on to sustain and uphold it. '"Why leave out the British Army? What's history without the Army, eh?"' Colonel Mayhew asks himself (*BA*: 141). '"[W]hy leave out the Army, as my husband was saying, if it's history?"' his wife later parrots (*BA*: 178), while another imagines how she herself would organise a finale: 'a Grand Ensemble. Army; Navy; Union Jack; and behind them perhaps – Mrs Mayhew sketched what she would have done had it been her pageant – the Church. In cardboard' (161).

In *Three Guineas* Woolf yet imagines the creation of a Society of Outsiders, whose purpose would be to undermine national jingoism, refuse the honouring of violence and work for peace and harmony. The women who form this society, she declares, will not endorse masculine patriotic rhetoric:

> When he says, as history proves that he has said, and may say again, 'I am fighting to protect our country' and thus seeks to rouse her patriotic emotion, she will ask herself, 'What does "our country" mean to me an outsider?' To do this she will analyse the meaning of patriotism in her own case. She will inform herself of the position of her sex and her class in the past. She will inform herself of the amount of land, wealth and property in the possession of her own sex and class in the present – how much of 'England' in fact belongs to her. (*AROO*: 311)

It is in the social, economic and political sense that Woolf declares, 'as a woman, I have no country'. A woman's feeling for her country, Woolf suggests, may be stirred 'by the cawing of rooks in an elm tree, by the splash of waves on a beach, or by English voices murmuring nursery rhymes', but it results not in a feeling of national superiority but the wish 'to give to England first what she desires of peace and freedom for the whole world' (*AROO*: 313).

Woolf's argument in *Three Guineas* is that in order to do so women must practice 'indifference', ignoring displays of patriotic emotion and 'national self-praise' as they would a child strutting for attention (314). The same principle of struggle between a masculine politics of primitive, childlike violence and a feminine politics of domestic indifference is transferred to the marriage of the Olivers in *Between the Acts*. While Giles stamps a snake and a toad to death ('it was action. Action relieved him'; 89), Isa abhors the small violent acts by which her husband asserts his masculinity and studiously ignores his attitude of civilised, patriarchal superiority:

> She had not spoken to him, not one word. Nor looked at him either. . . . Giles then did what to Isa was his little trick; shut his lips; frowned; and took up the pose of one who bears the burden of the world's woe, making money for her to spend.
>
> 'No,' said Isa, as plainly as words could say it. 'I don't admire you,' and looked, not at his face, but at his feet. 'Silly little boy, with blood on his boots.' (*BA*: 100)

The English landscape in *Between the Acts* is something that Woolf imagines continuing both before and after human existence, bearing the scars of its use under ancient Britons, Romans, Elizabethans and the Napoleonic wars, to which the present-day cesspool (another figural image of the garbage of imperial history) makes its own brief addition. The elderly Mrs Lucy Swithin, reading Wells' *Outline of History*, learns of the 'pre-history' of the earth before man's existence, an incomprehensibly distant past in which there were 'rhododendron forests in Piccadilly; when the entire continent, not then, she understood, divided by a channel, was all one' (*BA*: 8). Resisting the conventional model of a progressive history centred on the existence of mankind, Lucy regards the past, present and future as at once continuous and cyclical. '"I don't believe . . . that there ever were such people"', she says when asked if the Victorians had really been as they were portrayed in the pageant, '"[o]nly you and me and William dressed differently"' (156).

Woolf had written of her conception of the novel in April 1938, '[l]et it be random & tentative . . . don't, I implore, lay down a scheme; call in all the cosmic immensities; & force my tired and diffident brain to embrace another whole'. Avoiding the considered theorising that had made the writing of Bernard's final soliloquy in *The Waves* so exhausting, in *Between the Acts* she expresses similar ideas in Lucy Swithin's serene contemplation of the discordant elements of existence ultimately 'producing harmony – if not to us, to a gigantic ear attached to a gigantic head', and the Reverend Streatfield's hesitant interpretation of the pageant as implying that 'we are members one of another. Each is part of the whole' (172). While the religious Mrs Swithin is content in the belief that the underlying harmony of the universe will reveal itself in a spiritual afterlife, the Reverend yet charges his listeners with striving towards it in the here and now. '"Dare we"', he asks, as fighter planes move in ominous formation overhead, '"limit life to ourselves? May we not hold that there is a spirit that inspires, pervades"' . . . '"Scraps, orts and fragments! Surely we should unite?"' (173). It is this bringing together of the separate, self-conscious selves of the audience ('*Dispersed are we*', the gramophone accompaniment intones throughout the performance), if only for a moment, that is Miss LaTrobe's artistic vision. With the pageant over, however, it fades rapidly into a sense of failure and the urge to create anew. Inspired by the appearance of the English landscape as the dark of night descends, making it 'land merely, no land in particular' (189), she begins to conceive her next play: 'Words rose . . . . Words without meaning – wonderful words' (191). In an essay titled 'Craftmanship', written for a radio broadcast in 1937, Woolf herself had commented on the continuity of past and present inherent in the medium of language: 'Words, English words, are full of echoes, of memories, of associations – naturally. They have been out and about, on people's lips, in their houses, in the streets, in the fields, for many centuries.' She was still pushing the boundaries of fiction's ability to express the reality of existence: 'How can we combine the old words in new orders so that they survive,' she asks herself, 'so that they create beauty, so that they tell the truth?'

SUMMARY

The early 1900s witnessed a paradigm shift in the metaphysics of space and time that pervaded scientific, philosophical and cultural discourse and quickly extended to the broader popular imagination, posing profound questions about the nature of the universe and the human subject within it. For many artists and intellectuals the theories of Bergson and Einstein, with their challenge to the mechanistic determinism of traditional ontological and scientific theories, dove-tailed with the broader cultural and psychological turn to relativized explanations of the world whose widespread circulation and effect were marking the first decades of the twentieth century. Science and art no longer seemed in opposition, but part of the same radical reframing of modern reality. Demonstrating that the workings of the universe were more random and the existence of things less solid than had previously been assumed, the new philosophy and the new physics resonated in both formal and conceptual ways with the new realism of the modern novel. Lending metaphoric force to its questioning of social and aesthetic norms and conventions, and offering a 'science' of the unknowable subjective mind and incomprehensible physical universe, they stimulated new ways of conceiving and representing in art the relation of physical and spiritual existence, and of the transience of immediate experience and the immensity of the distant past. The 'to the moment' emphasis of the modernist novel in the 1920s shifts accordingly over the 1930s to a concern with historical continuity, and the imagining of a modern art that does not so much break from its past as contain and evolve it. 'The whole of what is called "the past" is with me, seen anew, vividly', Dorothy Richardson wrote at the close of the final book of *Pilgrimage*, 'the past does not stand "being still". It moves, growing with one's growth' (*P* IV: 657).

AFTER JOYCE

That the novel had reached its apocalyptic end was a common assertion in the 1920s and 1930s. The Spanish philosopher and literary critic José Ortega y Gasset, writing two years after Eliot's assertion in 1923 that *Ulysses* had signalled the end of the novel, similarly observed that modern innovations demonstrated the serious possibility that 'a literary genre may wear out'. The novel, he suggested, 'may be compared to a vast but finite quarry, in which [t]he workman of the primal hour had no trouble finding new blocks – new characters, new themes', but writers in the present day 'face the fact that only narrow and concealed veins are left them' (Ortega y Gasset, 1948: 57–8). The result was not only that the narrative perspective and thematic focus of the novel had contracted, but that the very act of 'quarrying' had become more conscious and meticulous. As Bernard Bergonzi writes of the perception of the novel at this time, *Ulysses* (he also cites Proust's *A la recherché du temps perdu*) 'mark the apotheosis of the realistic novel, where the minute investigation of human behaviour in all its aspects – physical, psychological and moral – is taken as far as it can go, while remaining within the bounds of coherence' (Bergonzi, 1970: 18).

By the 1940s a backlash against the subjective perspective and formal and linguistic experimentalism of the modernist novel had set in, propounded by Cambridge scholar F. R. Leavis (1895–1978) and his journal

Scrutiny, and the long influence of his critical philosophy that great literature should be a moral and spiritual study of human life. Leavis' classic study of the English novel, *The Great Tradition* (1948), cited Jane Austen, George Eliot, Henry James and Joseph Conrad as the major proponents of this kind of novel, writers who 'not only change the possibilities of the art for practitioners and readers, but . . . are significant in terms of that human awareness they promote; awareness of the possibilities of life' (Leavis, 1962: 10). The emphasis on 'human awareness' over the 'possibilities of art' reveals the implicit standard of realist comprehensibility that is fundamental to Leavis' ideal that literature convey moral values. Among the novelists of the early twentieth century, only D.H. Lawrence was similarly deemed to elevate common humanity over elitist artistry, 'his innovations and experiments [. . .] dictated by the most serious and urgent kind of interest in life' (35), in direct contrast to Joyce, for whom, Leavis had written in *Scrutiny* in 1933, 'the interest in words and their possibilities comes first' (Leavis, 1933: 194).

While Leavis concentrated on elevating Lawrence over Joyce as the most important novelist of the first half of the twentieth century, his wife Q. D. Leavis turned her attention to Woolf, whom she defined as a socially elitist and aesthetically mannered writer secluded within the rarefied ivory tower of upper-class Bloomsbury. The Leavisite influence was pervasive, establishing the literary canon and values that would underpin the teaching of English literature at all levels for the following three decades. For a post-war generation the internal focus of the modernist novel seemed socially and morally indefensible, the novelist Angus Wilson writing in the *Times Literary Supplement* in the early 1950s that,

> No sharpness of visual image, no increased sensibility, no deeper penetration of the individual consciousness, whether by verbal experiment or Freudian analysis, could fully atone for the frivolity of ignoring man as a social being, for treating personal relationships and subjective sensation in a social void. (Wilson, 1958: viii)

For Wilson, as Lawrence himself had similarly complained, this preoccupation with individual, subjective experience was redolent of the 'intellectual and emotional separateness from responsible society at large which most people experience so fully as adolescents' (viii).

Joyce's reputation was rescued from the anti-avant-gardism of literary criticism in the 1940s and 1950s by the work of Richard Ellmann and Hugh Kenner (Ellmann, 1982; Kenner, 1955), and following swiftly after, the burgeoning colossus of post-structuralist theory (Heath, 1972; MacCabe, 1979), with its re-reading of conventional realism as socially reactionary and experimental modernism as textually political. With the rise of the women's movement and the feminist critique of the gendered politics of the literary canon, Woolf and Richardson were rediscovered as significant figures within the history of both modernism and women's writing, even though, because of the largely realist ideology of Anglo-American feminist literary criticism, their perception as writers whose concerns were predominantly stylistic rather than social or political was still not yet substantially challenged (Showalter, 1977; Hanscombe, 1982; Hanscombe and Smyers, 1987). For Woolf this changed dramatically when critics such as Jane Marcus and Alex Zwerdling took vehement issue with the 'aestheticist' reading of her work and ideology. 'Why has Virginia Woolf's strong interest in realism, history, and the social matrix been largely ignored?', Zwerdling demanded at the start of his polemically titled *Virginia Woolf and the Real World* (1986), '[w]hy has it taken us so long to understand the importance of these elements in her work?' (Zwerdling, 1986: 15). At the same time a retreat from abstract theory and the insights of post-colonial criticism has witnessed the emergence of a similarly re-historicised, 'Irish' rather than 'Continental', Joyce (Kiberd, 1995; Nolan, 1995; Attridge and Howes, 2000; Gibson, 2002).

In the twenty-first century Joyce and Woolf probably have more 'consumers' than readers. Within the heritage industry Joyce has been repatriated as Ireland's prodigal son, to become the marketable cultural figurehead of a Europeanised nation and cosmopolitan capital, a phenomenon that would probably delight the writer himself (Bloom after all is an advertising salesman), not least for the purposes of vicious parody. Woolf is a heroine of feminist sexual and textual politics. The Irish Joyce and feminist Woolf possess an iconic relevance in contemporary culture that extends far beyond those who have actually read their work – in 2004 the Dublin celebrations for the centenary of Bloomsday (16 June) extended over five months, while the actress Nicole Kidman played a rather dour Virginia Woolf, complete with prosthetic nose, in the film *The*

Hours. By contrast Dorothy Richardson's reputation as a major innovator in the history of the novel has proved far less resilient. Her foreword to the 1938 collected edition was a belated appeal for public recognition of her role in forging a new pathway in fiction. Joining her on what was soon to become 'a populous highway', she recalls, two figures stood out: 'One a woman mounted upon a magnificently caparisoned charger, the other a man walking, with eyes devoutly closed, weaving as he went a rich garment of new words wherewith to clothe the antique dark material of his engrossment' (*P* I: 10). She does not need to name them. Joyce and Woolf were already the acknowledged exemplars of the 'modernist' novel, while Richardson's massive, mutating, endless record of a life's worth of impressions had been all but forgotten.

Unassimilated by received critical opinion, *Pilgrimage* continues to problematise the tenets by which the 'modernist novel' has traditionally been defined, refusing to subdue the expression of life to the form of art. 'What is called "creation" imaginative transformation, fantasy, invention," Richardson wrote at the end of *Pilgrimage* 'is only based on reality' (*P* IV: 657). 'Can anything produced by man be called "creation"?', she continued, '[t]he incense burners do not seem to know that in acclaiming what they call "a work of genius" they are recognising what is potentially within themselves' (657). Artistic creation, for Joyce, Woolf and Richardson, involved the collaboration of the artist *and* the reader. 'Though people may read more into *Ulysses* than I ever intended, who is to say that they are wrong', Joyce once asked, 'do any of us know what we are creating?' (Power, 1999: 102–3).

NOTES

SERIES EDITOR'S PREFACE

1   The sections in the *Little Review* all appeared under their Homeric titles: 'Telemachus', 'Nestor', 'Proteus', 'Calypso', 'Lotus-Eaters', 'Hades', 'Aeolus', 'Lestrygonians', 'Scylla and Charybdis', 'The Wandering Rocks', 'Sirens', 'Cyclops', 'Nausicaa' (the remaining unpublished sections were 'Oxen of the Sun', 'Circe', 'Eumaeus', 'Ithaca', 'Penelope'). These were later substituted by numbers when *Ulysses* was published in book form in 1922.

2   The first eleven books of Pilgrimage were published separately: *Pointed Roofs* (1915), *Backwater* (1916), *Honeycomb* (1917), *The Tunnel* (Feb. 1919), *Interim* (Dec. 1919; also serialised in the *Little Review*, June 1919–May 1920), *Deadlock* (1921), *Revolving Lights* (1923), *The Trap* (1925), *Oberland* (1927), *Dawn's Left Hand* (1931), *Clear Horizon* (1935). The twelfth, *Dimple Hill*, was added to the four-volume collected edition *Pilgrimage* (London: Dent; New York: Knopf, 1938). A thirteenth, *March Moonlight*, which Richardson had been working on up to her death, appeared in the revised edition published by Dent in 1967.

FURTHER READING

AFTER JOYCE, RICHARDSON AND WOOLF

Connor, S. (1996) *James Joyce*, Plymouth: Northcote House.
   Concise yet cutting-edge critical introduction from the *Writers and Their Work* series.

Deming. R. (1970) *James Joyce: The Critical Heritage*, London: Routledge and Kegan Paul.
   Again essential reading, the *Critical Heritage* series collects together contemporary reviews, essays, letters and diary entries on a writer and his or her work, allowing the present-day reader to understand the climate of opinion within which the writing was originally produced and received. The Joyce edition is published in two volumes, covering the years 1907–27 and 1928–41 respectively.

Ellmann, R. ([1959] 1982) *James Joyce*, Oxford: Oxford University Press.
   Ellmann's colossal study remains the authoritative biography, as epitomised by its opening sentence: 'We are still learning to be James Joyce's contemporaries, to understand our interpreter.'

Gilbert, S. (1930) *James Joyce's 'Ulysses'*, London: Faber.
   Another essential read, this challenging but indispensable guide to *Ulysses*, which published the famous 'schema' for the first time, was written under Joyce's own direction by his friend Stuart Gilbert.

Henke, S. and Unkeless, E. (eds) (1982) *Women in Joyce*, Brighton: Harvester.
   One of the key early Anglo-American feminist literary critical studies of Joyce, this collection of essays offers a generally positive reading of his view of women and representation of female characters.

Kenner, H. (1955) *Dublin's Joyce*, London: Chatto and Windus.
   More challenging in style and focus than Ellmann's biography but equally rewarding, Kenner's critical analysis was the other seminal Joyce study of the 1950s.

Kime Scott, B. (1984) *Joyce and Feminism*, Brighton: Harvester.
   Kime Scott usefully articulates her own definition and application of a feminist perspective to Joyce and his work, as well as identifying a historical framework of feminist readings of Joyce from the 1910s to the 1980s.

Lawrence, K. (1990) 'Joyce and Feminism' in Attridge (ed.) *The Cambridge Companion to James Joyce*, Cambridge: Cambridge University Press.
   A useful introductory essay mapping the key trends within feminist Joyce scholarship.

Levin, H. ([1941] 1960) *James Joyce: A Critical Introduction*, London: Faber.
   One of the first critical books on Joyce, of its time but immensely readable, situating *Ulysses* within the narrative tradition of the modern novel.

MacCabe, C. (1979; 2nd ed. 2002) *James Joyce and the Revolution of the Word*, Basingstoke: Macmillan.
   Challenging yet influential study arguing for the politics of language in Joyce's work. The second edition includes four additional essays.

Power, A. ([1974] 1999) *Conversations with James Joyce*, Dublin: Lilliput Press.
   Power's fascinating transcription of his conversations with Joyce in

Paris in the 1920s, covering a range of topics from Joyce's thoughts about his own work and that of other writers, to issues of religion, politics and aesthetics more generally.

WORKS ON DOROTHY RICHARDSON

Bluemel, K. (1997) *Experimenting on the Borders of Modernism: Dorothy Richardson's 'Pilgrimage'*, Athens, Ga.: University of Georgia Press.
    A detailed feminist critical reading of *Pilgrimage* and Richardson's significance as a modernist writer.

Brimley Johnson, R. (1920) *Some Contemporary Novelists (Women)*, London: Leonard Parsons.
    Fascinating for being probably the earliest full-length critical study of women writers in the first decades of the twentieth century, this includes a chapter on the first five books of *Pilgrimage*.

Bronfen, E. (1999) *Dorothy Richardson's Art of Memory: Space, Identity, Text*, Manchester: Manchester University Press.
    First published in German in 1986, Bronfen's important book signalled a new direction in Richardson studies, moving away from the traditional feminist literary critical focus on questions of the 'gender of modernism' to explore the phenomenology of material and imaginary spaces as played out across Richardson's representation of real and psychological landscapes in *Pilgrimage*.

Buchanan, A. (2000) 'Dorothy Miller Richardson: A Bibliography 1900 to 1999' *Journal of Modern Literature* 24:1, 135-60.
    Invaluable bibliography listing all of Richardson's own fictional and non-fictional writing, as well as subsequent reviews and scholarship.

Fromm, G. G. (1977) *Dorothy Richardson: A Biography*, Urbana: University of Illinois Press.
    Useful critical biography, demonstrating the parallels between Richardson's life and that of her autobiographical protagonist Miriam Henderson.

Hanscombe, G. (1982) *The Art of Life: Dorothy Richardson and the Development of Feminist Consciousness*, London: Owen.

Landmark feminist study that first recuperated Richardson from almost total critical neglect.

Kime Scott, B. (ed.) (1990) *The Gender of Modernism*, Bloomington: Indiana University Press.

Kime Scott's indispensable anthology of work by modernist women writers includes several of Richardson's most important critical essays, as well as May Sinclair's 1918 review 'The Novels of Dorothy Richardson'.

Mepham, J. (2000) 'Dorothy Richardson's "Unreadability": Graphic Style and Narrative Strategy in a Modernist Novel', *English Literature in Transition* 43:4, 449–64.

A fascinating essay that draws attention to the changing graphic style, as well as offering stimulating suggestions as to the reasons for and significance of this, within the *Pilgrimage* books.

Radford, J. (1991) *Dorothy Richardson*, London: Harvester Wheatsheaf.

Excellent concise introduction to Richardson and her work.

Thomson, G. H. (1996) *A Reader's Guide to Dorothy Richardson's 'Pilgrimage'*, Greensboro: ELT Press.

Thomson's reference guide sets out the chronology of events in *Pilgrimage* and details character relations and spatial contexts. It is accompanied by a selected annotated bibliography.

—— (1999) *Notes on 'Pilgrimage': Dorothy Richardson Annotated*, Greensboro: ELT Press.

Following on from the guide above, Thomson's notes detail the key cultural events, ideas, people and texts alluded to in the novel, and translates foreign words and phrases.

—— (2001) *The Editions of Dorothy Richardson's Pilgrimage: A Comparison of Texts*, Greensboro: ELT Press.

Watts, C. (1995) *Dorothy Richardson*, Plymouth: Northcote House.
Another rewarding introduction to Richardson's work in the *Writers and Their Work* series, drawing particular attention to her column for the avant-garde film journal *Close-Up* and its relevance for her literary aesthetics.

Winning, J. (2000) *The Pilgrimage of Dorothy Richardson*, Madison: University of Wisconsin Press.
Drawing on Richardson's letters and manuscript drafts, Winning argues persuasively for a concealed exploration of lesbian identity and desire within *Pilgrimage*.

WORKS ON VIRGINIA WOOLF

Beer, G. (1996) *Virginia Woolf: The Common Ground*, Edinburgh: Edinburgh University Press.
An absorbing and provocative collection of essays concentrating on conceptualisations of history in Woolf's work.

Black, N. (2003) *Virginia Woolf as Feminist*, New York: Cornell University Press.
Black offers a detailed and incisive critical study of Woolf's feminism and the writing of *Three Guineas*.

Lee, H. (1996) *Virginia Woolf*, London: Chatto and Windus.
The definitive critical biography.

Majumdar, R. and McLaurin, A. (1975) *Virginia Woolf: The Critical Heritage*, London: Routledge and Kegan Paul.
Another invaluable anthology of the contemporary critical reception of Woolf's novels and essay collections.

Marcus, L. (1995) *Virginia Woolf*, Plymouth: Northcote House.
The Woolf volume in the *Writers and their Work* series offers a critically stimulating and immensely readable account of Woolf's oeuvre, paying particular attention to the preoccupation with issues of history, memory

and narrative, the city, gender and sexuality, and biography and autobiography in her writings.

Moi, T. (1985) *Sexual / Textual Politics: Feminist Literary Theory*, London: Methuen.
Moi's comparison of the focus and methodologies of Anglo-American and French feminist literary criticism opens with a chapter on the critical reception of Virginia Woolf, taking specific issue with Elaine Showalter's ambivalent response to women modernist writers in *A Literature of Their Own* (below).

Naremore, J. (1973) *The World Without a Self: Virginia Woolf and the Novel*, New Haven: Yale University Press.
A detailed study of narrative strategy and interior monologue in Woolf's fiction.

Rose, S. and Sellars, S. (eds) (2000) *The Cambridge Companion to Virginia Woolf*, Cambridge: Cambridge University Press.
Another volume in the accessible *Cambridge Companion* series, this collection includes essays on all of Woolf's novels as well as her diaries and letters, along with assessments of her broader interest in aesthetics, psychoanalysis, feminism and politics.

Rosenberg, B. C. and Dubino, J. (eds) (1997) *Virginia Woolf and the Essay*, Basingstoke: Macmillan.
An excellent collection of essays on Woolf's work as a critic and essayist.

Showalter, E. ([1977]; 2003) *A Literature of Their Own: British Women Novelists from Brontë to Lessing*, London: Virago.
Showalter's classic of feminist literary studies is notoriously critical of the modernist aesthetics of both Woolf and Dorothy Richardson.

Silver, B. (2000) *Virginia Woolf: Icon*, Chicago: Chicago University Press.
A fascinating study of the reception of Woolf within both high and popular culture.

Whitworth, M. (2005) *Virginia Woolf*, Oxford: Oxford University Press.
A clear and lively introduction, combining biographical information with an examination of the key literary, cultural, scientific and philosophical contexts significant for understanding Woolf's work.

Zwerdling, A. (1986) *Virginia Woolf and the Real World*, Berkeley: University of California Press.
Groundbreaking study that argued against the long-standard reading of Woolf as an aesthete in a literary 'ivory tower', and drew attention to the significance of the themes of feminism, class, war and politics in her work.

INTERNET RESOURCES

www.jamesjoyce.ie
The James Joyce Centre, Dublin

www.english.osu.edu/organizations/ijjf/
The International James Joyce Foundation

www.utoronto.ca/IVWS/
The International Virginia Woolf Society

www.virginiawoolfsociety.co.uk/
The Virginia Woolf Society of Great Britain

www.uncg.edu/eng/elt/richardson/contents.htm
George H. Thompson's indispensable ebook *The Editions of Dorothy Richardson's Pilgrimage: A Companion of Texts*, ELT Press 2001.

WORKS CITED

References to Joyce, Woolf and Richardson's major fiction, critical essays, letters and autobiographical writings are cited parenthetically throughout the text by the abbreviations given below. All other references are cited by author and date.

JOYCE

Joyce, J. ([1914] 2000) *Dubliners*, Harmondsworth: Penguin. [*Du*]

([1916] 2000) *A Portrait of the Artist as a Young Man*, Harmondsworth: Penguin. [*PA*]

([1922] 2000) *Ulysses*, Harmondsworth: Penguin. [*U*]

([1939] 2000) *Finnegans Wake*, Harmondsworth: Penguin. [*FW*]

(1966) *Letters of James Joyce*, 3 vols, ed. Stuart Gilbert (1) and Richard Ellmann (2–3), London: Faber. [*LJJ*]

(2000) *Occasional, Critical and Political Writing*, Oxford: Oxford University Press. [*OCP*]

RICHARDSON

Richardson, D. (1915) *Pointed Roofs*, London: Duckworth.

([1938] 1979) *Pilgrimage*, 4 vols, London: Virago. [*P*]

(1989) *Journey to Paradise: Short Stories and Autobiographical Sketches*, ed. Trudi Tate, London: Virago. [*JP*]

(1995) *Windows on Modernism: Selected Letters of Dorothy Richardson*, ed. Gloria Glikin Fromm, Athens, Ga.: University of Georgia Press. [*LDR*]

WOOLF

Woolf, V. ([1915] 2001) *The Voyage Out*, Oxford: Oxford University Press. [*VO*]

([1919] 1999) *Night and Day*, Oxford: Oxford University Press. [*ND*]

([1922] 1999) *Jacob's Room*, Oxford: Oxford University Press. [*JR*]

([1925] 1998) *Mrs Dalloway*, Oxford: Oxford University Press. [*MD*]

([1927] 1998) *To the Lighthouse*, Oxford: Oxford University Press. [*TL*]

([1928] 1998) *Orlando*, Oxford: Oxford University Press. [*O*]

([1929; 1937] 1998) *A Room of One's Own* and *Three Guineas*, Oxford: Oxford University Press. [*AROO*]

([1931] 1998) *The Waves*, Oxford: Oxford University Press. [*W*]

([1937] 1999) *The Years*, Oxford: Oxford University Press. [*Y*]

([1940] 2003) *Roger Fry. A Biography*, London: Vintage. [*RF*]

([1941] 1998) *Between the Acts*, Oxford: Oxford University Press. [*BA*]

(1966–7) *Collected Essays*, 4 vols, London: Hogarth Press. [*CE*]

(1977–84) *The Diary of Virginia Woolf*, 5 vols, eds. Anne Olivier Bell and Andrew McNeillie, London: Hogarth Press. [*D*]

(1986–94) *The Essays of Virginia Woolf*, 4 vols, ed. Andrew McNeillie, London: Hogarth Press. [*E*]

(1979) *Women and Writing*, ed. Michèle Barrett, London: Women's Press. [*WW*]

(1989) *Moments of Being*, ed. Jeanne Schulkind, London: Grafton [*MB*]

(1992a) *A Woman's Essays*, ed. Rachel Bowlby, Harmondsworth: Penguin.

(1992b) *The Crowded Dance of Modern Life*, ed. Rachel Bowlby, Harmondsworth: Penguin.

(2001) *The Mark on the Wall and Other Short Fiction*, Oxford: Oxford University Press. [*MW*]

SECONDARY TEXTS

Armstrong, N. (1987) *Desire and Domestic Fiction: A Political History of the Novel*, New York: Oxford University Press.

Attridge, D. and Howes, M. (2000) *Semicolonial Joyce*, Cambridge: Cambridge University Press.

Auerbach, E. (1953) *Mimesis: The Representation of Reality in Western Literature*, Princeton, N.J.: Princeton University Press.

Banfield, A. (1982) *Unspeakable Sentences: Narration and Representation in the Language of Fiction*, London: Routledge and Kegan Paul.

Bazin, N. (1973) *Virginia Woolf and the Androgynous Vision*, New Brunswick: Rutgers University Press.

Beach, J. W. (1932) *The Twentieth Century Novel: Studies in Technique*, New York: Appleton Crofts.

Beja, M. (1992) *James Joyce: A Literary Life*, Basingstoke: Macmillan.

Belsey, C. (1980) *Critical Practice*, London: Methuen.

Bergonzi, B. (1970) *The Situation of the Novel*, London: Macmillan.

—— (1986) *The Myth of the Modern and Twentieth-Century Literature*, Brighton: Harvester.

Bergson, H. ([1910] 2001) *Time and Free Will: An Essay on the Immediate Data of Consciousness*, New York: Dover.

—— ([1911] 2004) *Matter and Memory*, New York: Dover.

Booth, W. C. (1961) *The Rhetoric of Fiction*, Chicago: University of Chicago Press.

Bowlby, R. (1988) *Feminist Destinations*, Oxford: Blackwell.

Bradbury, M. and McFarlane, J. (1976) *Modernism 1890–1930*, Harmondsworth: Penguin.

Brooker, J. (2004) *Joyce's Critics: Transitions in Reading and Culture*, Madison: University of Wisconsin Press.

Brooks, P. (1985) *Reading for the Plot: Design and Intention in Narrative*, New York: Vintage.

Brosnan, L. (1997) *Reading Virginia Woolf's Essays and Journalism: Breaking the Surface of Silence*, Edinburgh: Edinburgh University Press.

Budgen, F. (1972) *James Joyce and the Making of "Ulysses" and Other Writings*, London: Oxford University Press.

Cixous, H. (1968) *The Exile of James Joyce*, trans. S. Purcell, London: John Calder.

Cohn, D. (1978) *Transparent Minds: Narrative Modes for Presenting Consciousness in Fiction*, Princeton: Princeton University Press.

Conrad. J. (1986), *The Collected Letters of Joseph Conrad, Vol 2: 1898–1902*, eds. F. R. Karl and L. Davies, Cambridge: Cambridge University Press.

Cuddy-Keane, M. (2003) *Virginia Woolf, the Intellectual, and the Public Sphere*, Cambridge: Cambridge University Press.

Dainton, B. (2000) *Stream of Consciousness: Unity and Continuity in Conscious Experience*, London: Routledge.

Doody, M. A. (1996) *The True Story of the Novel*, New Brunswick: Rutgers University Press.

Dusinberre, J. (1997) *Virginia Woolf's Renaissance: Woman Reader or Common Reader?*, Basingstoke: Macmillan.

Eagleton, T. (2005) *The English Novel*, Oxford: Blackwell.

Edel, L. (1955) *The Psychological Novel 1900–1950*, London: Hart-Davies.

Eysteinsson, A. (1990) *The Concept of Modernism*, New York: Cornell University Press.

Faulkner, P. (1977) *Modernism*, London: Methuen.

—— (ed.) (1986) *A Modernist Reader: Modernism in England 1910–1930*, London: Batsford.

Forster, E. M. (1927) *Aspects of the Novel*, London: Edward Arnold.

Frank, J. (1963) *The Widening Gyre: Crisis and Mastery in Modern Literature*, Bloomington: Indiana University Press.

Friedman, A. J. and Donley, C. (1985) *Einstein as Myth and Muse*, Cambridge: Cambridge University Press.

Friedman, M. J. (1955) *Stream of Consciousness: A Study of Literary Method*, New Haven: Yale University Press.

Furst, L. (ed.) (1992) *Realism*, London: Longman.

Gasiorek, A. (1995) *Post-War British Fiction: Realism and After*, London: Edward Arnold.

Genette, G. (1980) *Narrative Discourse: An Essay in Method*, trans. J. Lewin, New York: Cornell University Press.

Gibson, A. (2002) *Joyce's Revenge: History, Politics and Aesthetics in 'Ulysses'*, Oxford: Oxford University Press.

Gilbert, S. M. and Gubar, S. (1988–94) *No Man's Land: The Place of the Woman Writer in the Twentieth Century*, 3 vols, New Haven: Yale University Press.

Goldberg, S. L. (1961) *The Classical Temper: A Study of James Joyce's 'Ulysses'*, London: Chatto and Windus.

Goldman, J. (2001) *The Feminist Aesthetics of Virginia Woolf: Modernism, Post-Impressionism and the Politics of the Visual*, Cambridge: Cambridge University Press.

—— (2004) *Modernism, 1910–1945: Image to Apocalypse*, Basingstoke: Palgrave.

Groden, M. (1977) *'Ulysses' in Progress*, Princeton: Princeton University Press.

Gualtieri, E. (2000) *Virginia Woolf's Essays: Sketching the Past*, Basingstoke: Macmillan.

Hanscombe, G. and Smyers, V. (1987) *Writing for Their Lives: The Modernist Women, 1910–1940*, London: Women's Press, 1987.

Hart, C. (ed.) (1974) *Conversations with James Joyce*, New York: Barnes and Noble Books.

Heath, S. (1972) *The Nouveau Roman: A Study in the Practice of Writing*, London: Elek.

Heilbrun, C. (1973) *Towards a Recognition of Androgyny*, New York: Knopf.

Henke, S. (1990) *James Joyce and the Politics of Desire*, London: Routledge.

Herman, L. (1996) *Concepts of Realism*, Columbia, S.C.: Camden House.

Holtby, W. (1978) *Virginia Woolf: A Critical Memoir*, Chicago: Academy Press.

Humphrey, R. (1954) *Stream of Consciousness in the Modern Novel*, Berkeley: University of California Press.

Hynes, S. (1990) *A War Imagined: The First World War and English Culture*, London: Bodley Head.

James, H. (1934) *The Art of the Novel*, ed. R. P. Blackmur, New York: Scribner's.

—— (1956) *The Future of the Novel: Essays on the Art of Fiction*, ed. L. Edel, New York: Vintage.

—— (1984) *Letters of Henry James, Vol 4: 1895–1916*, ed. L. Edel, London: Belknap Press.

James, W. ([1890] 1981) *The Principles of Psychology*, Cambridge, Mass.: Harvard University Press.

Kennedy, J. B. (2003) *Space, Time and Einstein: An Introduction*, Chesham: Acumen.

Kermode, F. (1967) *The Sense of an Ending: Studies in the Theory of Fiction*, Oxford: Oxford University Press.

Kern, S. (1983) *The Culture of Time and Space 1880–1918*, Cambridge, Mass.: Harvard University Press.

Kiberd, D. (1995) *Inventing Ireland: The Literature of the Modern Nation*, London: Jonathan Cape.

Kime Scott, B. (1987) *James Joyce*, Brighton: Harvester.

—— (ed.) (1990) *The Gender of Modernism*, Bloomington: Indiana University Press.

—— (1995) *Refiguring Modernism 1: The Women of 1928* and *2: Postmodern Feminist Readings of Woolf, West and Barnes*, Bloomington: Indiana University Press.

Kumar, S. (1959) 'Dorothy Richardson and the Dilemma of "Being versus Becoming"', *Modern Language Notes* 74:6, 494–501.

LaCapra, D. (1987) *History, Politics, and the Novel*, New York: Cornell University Press.

Lawrence, K. (1981) *The Odyssey of Style in 'Ulysses'*, Princeton: Princeton University Press.

Leavis, F. R. (1933) *For Continuity*, Cambridge: The Minority Press.

—— (1948) *The Great Tradition: George Eliot, Henry James, Joseph Conrad*, London: Chatto and Windus.

Levenson, M. (1984) *A Genealogy of Modernism*, Cambridge: Cambridge University Press.

—— (ed.) (1999) *The Cambridge Companion to Modernism*, Cambridge: Cambridge University Press.

Levine, G. (1981) *The Realistic Imagination: English Fiction from Frank to Lady Chatterley*, London: University of Chicago Press.

—— (ed.) *Realism and Representation: Essays on the Problem of Realism in Relation to Science, Literature, and Culture*, Madison: University of Wisconsin Press.

Lewis, W. ([1927] 1993) *Time and Western Man*, Santa Rosa: Black Sparrow Press.

Lodge, D. (1977) *The Modes of Modern Writing: Metaphor, Metonymy and the Typology of Modern Literature*, London: Edward Arnold.

Lorentz, H. A., Einstein, A., Minkowski, H., and Weyl, H. (1952) *The Principle of Relativity: A Collection of Original Memoirs on the Special and General Theory of Relativity*, New York: Dover Press.

Lubbock, P. (1921) *The Craft of Fiction*, London: Cape.

Lukács, G. ([1920] 1989) *The Historical Novel*, London: Merlin.

Madox Ford, F. (1947), *The March of Literature: From Confucius to Modern Times*, London: George Allen and Unwin.

—— (2003), 'On Impressionism', repr. in *The Good Soldier*, eds. K. Womack and W. Baker, Ontario: Broadview Press.

Mahaffey, V. (1988) *Reauthorizing Joyce*, Cambridge: Cambridge University Press.

Matz, J. (2001) *Literary Impressionism and Modernist Aesthetics*, Cambridge: Cambridge University Press.

Minow-Pinkney, M. (1987) *Virginia Woolf & the Problem of the Subject: Feminine Writing in the Major Novels*, New Brunswick: Rutgers University Press.

Morris, P. (2003) *Realism*, London: Routledge.

Nicholls, P. (1995) *Modernisms: A Literary Guide*, Basingstoke: Macmillan.

Nolan, E. (1995) *James Joyce and Nationalism*, London: Routledge.

North, M. (1999) *Reading 1922: A Return to the Scene of the Modern*, Oxford: Oxford University Press.

Ortega y Gasset, J. ([1925] 1948) *The Dehumanization of Art and Ideas about the Novel*, Princeton: Princeton University Press.

Parrinder, P. and Philmus, R. (1980) *H. G. Wells' Literary Criticism*, Brighton: Harvester.

Peters, J. (2001) *Conrad and Impressionism*, Cambridge: Cambridge University Press.

Potts, W. (ed.) (1979) *Portraits of the Artist in Exile: Recollections of James Joyce by Europeans*, Seattle: University of Washington Press.

Pykett, L. (1995) *Engendering Fictions: The English Novel in the Early Twentieth Century*, London: Arnold.

Rice, T. J. (1997) *Joyce, Chaos, and Complexity*, Urbana: University of Illinois Press.

Rosenberg, B. C. (1995) *Virginia Woolf and Samuel Johnson: Common Readers*, Basingstoke: Macmillan.

Schwarz, D. R. (1986) *The Humanistic Heritage: Critical Theories of the English Novel from James to Hillis Miller*, Basingstoke: Macmillan.

Sherry, V. (2003) *The Great War and the Language of Modernism*, Oxford: Oxford University Press.

Spencer, J. (1986) *The Rise of the Woman Novelist: From Aphra Behn to Jane Austen*, Oxford: Blackwell.

Spoo, R. E. (1994) *James Joyce and the Language of History: Dedalus's Nightmare*, New York: Oxford University Press.

Stevenson, W. (1996) *Romanticism and the Androgynous Sublime*, Madison: Fairleigh Dickinson University Press.

Strawson, G. (1994) *Mental Reality*, Cambridge, Mass.: MIT Press.

Stubbs, P. (1979) *Women and Fiction, 1880–1920*, Brighton: Harvester.

Tate, T. (1998) *Modernism, History and the First World War*, Manchester: Manchester University Press.

Van Ghent, D. (1953) *The English Novel: Form and Function*, New York: Rinehart and Company.

Watt, I. (1957) *The Rise of the Novel: Studies in Defoe, Richardson, and Fielding*, London: Chatto and Windus.

Whitworth, M. H. (2002) *Einstein's Wake: Relativity, Metaphor, and Modernist Literature*, Oxford: Oxford University Press.

Williams, R. (1970) *The English Novel from Dickens to Lawrence*, London: Chatto and Windus.

Wilson, A. (1958) 'Diversity and Depth', *Times Literary Supplement*, 15th August.

INDEX

THE NEW CRITICAL IDIOM
Series Editor: John Drakakis, University of Stirling

The New Critical Idiom is an invaluable series of introductory guides to today's critical terminology. Each book:

- provides a handy, explanatory guide to the use (and abuse) of the term
- offers an original and distinctive overview by a leading literary and cultural critic
- relates the term to the larger field of cultural representation

With a strong emphasis on clarity, lively debate and the widest possible breadth of examples, *The New Critical Idiom* is an indispensable approach to key topics in literary studies.

> 'Easily the most informative and wide-ranging series of its kind, so packed with bright ideas that it has become an indispensable resource for students of literature.'
>
> Terry Eagleton, *University of Manchester*

Available in this series:

For further information on individual books in the series, visit:
www.routledge.com/literature/nci

Routledge Guides to Literature*

Editorial Advisory Board: Richard Bradford (University of Ulster at Coleraine), Jan Jedrzejewski (University of Ulster at Coleraine), Duncan Wu (St. Catherine's College, University of Oxford).

Routledge Guides to Literature offer clear introductions to the most widely studied authors and literary texts. Each book engages with texts, contexts and criticism, highlighting the range of critical views and contextual factors that need to be taken into consideration in advanced studies of literary works. The series encourages informed but independent readings of texts by ranging as widely as possible across the contextual and critical issues relevant to the works examined and highlighting areas of debate as well as those of critical consensus. Alongside general guides to texts and authors, the series includes 'sourcebooks', which allow access to reprinted contextual and critical materials as well as annotated extracts of primary text.

A selection of titles available in this series:

*Some books in this series were originally published in the Routledge Literary Sourcebooks series, edited by Duncan Wu, or the Complete Critical Guide to English Literature series, edited by Richard Bradford and Jan Jedrzejewski.

A full listing of the series can be found at www.routledge/literature/series

Related titles from Routledge

The Postmodern
Simon Malpas

the NEW CRITICAL IDIOM

How can one understand the nature of the present?
What might it mean to say the world has become postmodern?

Simon Malpas investigates the theories and definitions of postmodernism and postmodernity, and explores their impact in such areas as identity, history, art, literature and culture. In attempting to locate the essence of the postmodern, and the contrasting experiences of postmodernity in the Western and developing worlds, he looks closely at:

- modernism and postmodernism
- modernity and postmodernity
- subjectivity
- history
- politics

This useful guidebook will introduce students to a range of key thinkers who have sought to question the contemporary situation, and will enable readers to begin to approach the primary texts of postmodern theory and culture with confidence.

ISBN10: 0-415-28064-8 (hbk)
ISBN10: 0-415-28065-6 (pbk)
ISBN13: 978-0-415-28064-8 (hbk)
ISBN13: 978-0-415-28065-5 (pbk)

Available at all good bookshops
For further information on our literature series, please visit:
www.routledge.com/literature/series.asp

For ordering and further information please visit:
www.routledge.com

Related titles from Routledge

The New Bloomsday Book
A Guide Through Ulysses
Harry Blamires

Third Edition

'This will become the standard work of its kind... Harry Blamires has written a straightforward, unpretentious 263-page paraphrase labour of love. Severely restricting flights of interpretation to useful cross-references, he stays close to the text at all times.' – *The Guardian*

Since 1966 readers new to James Joyce have depended upon this essential guide to Ulysses. Harry Blamires helps readers to negotiate their way through this formidable, remarkable novel and gain an understanding of it which, without help, it might have taken several readings to achieve.

The New Bloomsday Book is a crystal clear, page-by-page, line-by-line running commentary on the plot of Ulysses which illuminates symbolic themes and structures along the way. It is a highly accessible, indispensible guide for anyone reading Joyce's masterpiece for the first time.

To ensure that Blamires' classic work will remain useful to new readers, this third edition contains the page numbering and references to three commonly read editions of *Ulysses*.

ISBN10: 0-415-13857-4 (hbk)
ISBN10: 0-415-13858-2 (pbk)
ISBN13: 978-0-415-13857-4 (hbk)
ISBN13: 978-0-415-13858-1 (pbk)

Available at all good bookshops
For further information on our literature series, please visit:
www.routledge.com/literature/series.asp

For ordering and further information please visit:
www.routledge.com